FASHION IN FILM

For Mum & Dad

LAURENCE KING

This paperback edition first published
in Great Britain in 2021 by

Laurence King Student & Professional
An imprint of Quercus Editions Ltd
Carmelite House
50 Victoria Embankment
London EC4Y 0DZ

An Hachette UK company

Reprinted in 2021

A CIP catalogue record for this book is available
from the British Library

TPB ISBN 978-1-78627-709-1

10 9 8 7 6 5 4 3

Designed by Sarah Schrauwen

Printed and bound in China by C&C Offset Ltd.

MIX
Paper from
responsible sources
FSC® C008047

Papers used by Quercus are from well-managed forests
and other responsible sources.

Front cover Audrey Hepburn wearing Givenchy
in *Breakfast at Tiffany's* (see page 108)
Back cover Left: Olga Kurylenko wearing Prada
in *Quantum of Solace* (see page 166); top right:
Catherine Deneuve wearing Yves Saint Laurent in
Mississippi Mermaid (see page 216); bottom right:
Robert Redford wearing Ralph Lauren in *The Great
Gatsby* (see page 174)

Acknowledgements
Jill Burgess-Grider, Kevin Conran, Betsy Heimann,
Lindy Hemming, Michael Kaplan, Donna Karan,
Gilly Laverty, Judianna Makovsky, Ellen Mirojnick,
Bart Mueller, Sandy Powell, Mary Quant, Kurt Swanson,
Amy Westcott, Michael Wilkinson, Janty Yates

CHRISTOPHER LAVERTY

FASHION
IN FILM

CONTENTS

Fashion in film – does it even exist? Some might argue no, that the very phrase is redundant. After all, everything we see worn on screen is, by definition, costume. Yet that is too simplistic a concept. If costume only becomes fashion away from the screen, what happens when we return? When we look at the meaning and impact of costume on the world of fashion alongside its intentional role of bringing characters to life? Then we have distance, the ability to combine fashion and costume as a cultural fixture.

This book concentrates solely on the work of fashion designers that have created clothing for film, or in some cases vice versa – those who have worked in costume and then become fashion designers – but the overall rationale is that the designer must have functioned in both industries during their career. This is to aid scope. It became apparent during my initial research that writing an entire book about how fashion has been affected by clothes on screen is a different publication entirely. I wanted to keep this title distinct and focused.

Narrowing down which designers and which films to focus on was, to be a honest, a nightmare – so many to include and only a limited amount of space. How to choose? For starters, a featured designer, or house, must have designed specifically for the film being analyzed. I have considered shopped garments in each designer's individual profile, but ultimately I wanted clothing by fashion designers that is intentionally created as costume. This precludes certain designers that you might expect to see, such as Comme des Garçons, whom costume designer Aggie Gerard Rogers used for *Beetlejuice* (1988), or Zegna, who provided off-the-rack suits for George Clooney in *The American* (2010). The same goes for certain costumiers, like Bob Mackie, who designed for screen several times (*Pennies From Heaven*, 1981; *Staying Alive*, 1983) but is primarily known for stage wear. Even Orry-Kelly and William Travilla have been omitted, principally because they are costume designers who, bar a newswire column for Kelly and scattered collections for Travilla (including one for Grattan), influenced fashion rather than existed within the industry. For many the most surprising omission will be Edith Head. Head is certainly mentioned, particularly in regards to the Givenchy little black dress for *Breakfast at Tiffany's* (1961), but again, apart from some tie-in collections, she was a fashion tastemaker not a designer. Even with these strict criteria to narrow

the field, there just was not space to include everyone: Norma Kamali, for example, who designed gowns for the Emerald City portion of *The Wiz* (1978).

Other aspects of the fascinating world of fashion and film crossover include collaborations such as the unusual teaming of *Muppets* creator Jim Henson and fantasy illustrator Brian Froud for *The Dark Crystal* (1983). They produced a line of clothing based on costumes seen in the film that was sold through Liberty's of London. A similar idea was employed by Disney for *Oz the Great and Powerful* (2013), when footwear designer Steve Madden, among others, produced over 400 accessories inspired by the movie for the Home Shopping Network. Also several high-profile costume designers worked with Prada on their 'Iconoclasts' installations in 2015. But, however interesting these projects are, unless a major couture designer or their house was involved, and the garments were created specifically for cinema, they did not meet my mandate for this book.

Certain fashion designers were not included because the clothing they provided for a film was not deliberately designed or intended for it. Elie Saab is someone I wanted to feature, but as yet he has not created specifically for movies. His garments have been used – by costumiers Kurt Swanson and Bart Mueller for *Stoker* (2013), for example – but interpreted independently of a collaboration. The film *Prêt-à-Porter* (1994) is crammed full of fashion designers and their clothing, and I could have mentioned it in every other chapter, but it is a satirical piece, not focused on clothing as much as the industry. There would have been scant analysis to make.

With each profile I have attempted to channel the same investigative approach I employ with my website Clothes on Film. In general, I have discussed the career of the designer in question, their background, approach, and evolution, and then examined three or four of their films in detail. I am not looking only at the clothes themselves, but exploring what they mean in the context of the story being told. I also look at the garments' use as a potential marketing tool, their reverberations – if any – in the fashion world, and their legacy on both catwalk and screen. Occasionally, as in the case of Rodarte, for instance, I will break down only one film (i.e., *Black Swan*, 2010), because at the time of writing that is the designer's only contribution to cinema. So why include Rodarte if they have only designed for the

one movie? Because the story behind their involvement
is too sensational to ignore. So exceptions have been
made. You might also question why certain well-known
titles have been left out or skipped over in profiles
where you might be expecting to read more. While I
wanted to make sure the essentials were included –
classics like *The Wizard of Oz* (1939) and *Barbarella*
(1968) – I wanted to focus on content that has never
been published before, and to take the opportunity
to correct details that have been incorrectly reported
time and time again, such as Agnès B's contribution for
John Travolta in *Pulp Fiction* (1994). But you can read all
about that in the following pages. Don't let me keep you.

     As a final note, I would like to add that,
as an influence on fashion, I feel cinema functions
best within the realms of science fiction and fantasy or period productions. Costume designer Trish
Summerville's cowl scarf by Maria Dora for *The Hunger
Games: Catching Fire* (2013) segued beautifully into
Paris couture; the reverse happened with Sarah Burton
and Alexander McQueen's modified red ruffle dress for
the same movie. These looks can exist seamlessly away
from narrative context because they are not contemporary. We as consumers can blend the past with fantasy
on screen to create our future. Costume as fashion is
what we want it to be: whatever the intention, a dress
in a movie is just a dress in a movie until meaning is
ascribed. Away from the screen such meaning is completely subjective. That same dress, whether originally
worn by Audrey Hepburn as an escort or Olga Kurylenko
as a spy, is now exclusively ours.

Christopher Laverty

This Elie Saab dress, worn by Nicole Kidman's character
Evie in *Stoker*, was chosen for the film by costumiers Bart
Mueller and Kurt Swanson. Sketch by Bart Mueller

AGNÈS B

WHO ARE YOU, POLLY MAGGOO? (1966)
THE MODEL COUPLE (1977)
RESERVOIR DOGS (1992)
PULP FICTION (1994)
MY NAME IS HMMM... (2013)

Agnès B, real name Agnès Troublé, is an ardent supporter of independent cinema and now a film-maker herself

—
p8 Harvey Keitel's friendship with Agnès B encouraged the designer to donate one black suit for his role in *Reservoir Dogs*. Betsy Heimann's meagre costume budget for the film was $10,000

There is cool and there is Agnès B. The hippest name in fashion, Agnès is a film-maker, writer and costume designer. The Agnès B look is simple – or more accurately, it defines simplicity. With collections that are a throwback to the fifties' beatnik fixation on striped T-shirts, long coats, mismatched skirts, sweaters and long oversized coats, Agnès B has been making clothes since the sixties but had a huge resurgence in the nineties. Now, thanks to that particular decade's retro revival, the label is once again deciding the high-street silhouette. Spring/Summer 2014 in particular belonged to Agnès B; every young-fashion store from Topshop to H&M copied a look that, if Agnès did not invent, she certainly owns.

Agnès B (real name Agnès Troublé), along with another beloved French brand of the seventies, Cacharel, contributed to director William Klein's satire on mechanical consumerism, *The Model Couple* (*Le couple témoin*, 1977). Agnès had worked with Klein on the fashion spoof *Who Are You, Polly Maggoo? (Qui êtes-vous, Polly Maggoo?,* 1966) when she featured and subsequently popularized her signature block-stripe T-shirt. *The Model Couple* is hardly a fashion movie, but it makes unexpectedly shrewd observations on clothing as a means of subjugation. Anémone and André Dussollier play a married couple in their mid- to late

p10 top *Who Are You, Polly Maggoo?* is the most comprehensive showcase of Agnès B's signature block stripe on film

—

p10 bottom Sketch by Agnès B of her frequently replicated striped T-shirt, available since the late 1970s

—

p11 left *The Model Couple*'s plain jumpsuits are a subtle comment on the stagnant uniformity of fashion

—

p11 right This jumpsuit designed by Agnès B for Spring/Summer 2016 is a contemporary, more tailored update on those featured in *The Model Couple*

twenties who agree to take part in a nationalized experiment by the 'Ministry of the Future' to observe and manipulate their behaviour in controlled conditions. They are watched 24 hours a day in a purpose-built apartment to assess the potential needs of a utopian society (the film is set in 2000). Upon arrival, their personal effects are removed, they strip and are interviewed naked. Both are given white bodysuits with their initials labelled on the front and back. The bodysuits are all-in-one utility garments, along with crimson-red toe socks (a quirky Agnès B touch) and no shoes. Here the couple's costumes take on a note of individuality, if not from themselves then the very concept of clinical attire itself. Consequently they become a fashion statement. Remember, too, that we are not voyeurs in this experiment because the participants are aware they are being watched. We are spectators.

As the experiment takes its toll on the couple, they revolt with the help of a punk-styled band of terrorists, conveniently reflecting the eve of this movement in Europe. One of the teen terrorists arrives wearing a distinctive knitted red balaclava. This garment was later referenced in *Spring Breakers* (2012) as part of the girls' robbery disguises (with added 'My Little Pony' patch on the front). *Spring Breakers* was produced by Agnès B, which surely cannot be a coincidence. The oppressors in *The Model Couple* wear black (evil), their victims white (good). William Klein's film is

Costume designer Betsy Heimann added the leather lapel to this black Agnès B suit worn by John Travolta in *Pulp Fiction* to give the ensemble a rockabilly touch

Betsy Heimann used Agnès B to costume Uma Thurman's character Mia in *Pulp Fiction* as a 'female (Reservoir) Dog'.

no less subtle than *Who Are You, Polly Maggoo?*, though he is arguably more adept at predicting a monotonous future than satirizing eccentricities of the present.

In Stephen Frears's *The Grifters* (1990), Anjelica Huston's slinky con artist Lilly Dillon wears an Agnès B dress remade by costumier Mark Bridges in white gabardine. Huston suggested the garment when the original choice fell short after testing. On rare occasions such as this, an actor 'pushing' a favourite brand for their character can assist rather than hinder a costume designer's job.

Costume designer Betsy Heimann also used Agnès B in two of her most famous projects, both for director Quentin Tarantino: *Reservoir Dogs* (1992) and *Pulp Fiction* (1994). The budget was so tight on Tarantino's debut movie that to find identical black suits for the main cast in order to echo the French New Wave, Heimann had to cheat. Two of the Dogs are wearing black jeans instead of trousers, mismatched and with dark blue jackets. Once again a personal connection came in handy; main star and producer Harvey Keitel knew Agnès B socially, so was able to acquire a brand new black suit for the shoot. On *Pulp Fiction*, Heimann had a little more money but barely more time. Again via Harvey Keitel, she managed to procure the velvet collar coat and velvet collar jacket worn by Mia Wallace (Uma Thurman) and Vincent Vega's (John Travolta) date suit. The suit did not originally have the leather lapel but Heimann requested it be added to

fit with the rockabilly vibe of Vincent's bolo necktie. It was also remade in a larger size to fit the actor. Betsy Heimann continues to use Agnès B wherever possible today, praising the designer's willingness to support independent film.

Agnès B debuted as a writer/director with *My Name is Hmmm... (Je m'appelle Hmmm...,* 2013), the story of Céline (Lou-Lélia Demerliac), a withdrawn 11-year-old girl who leaves home after years of abuse. Agnès B did not act as costumier, instead hiring François Jugé, but two items of her clothing feature: a non-descript coat and red knitted sweater worn by Céline. Red is a vital colour throughout the film; it acts, as red often does, as a warning, foreshadowing both real and conceivable dangers. Céline runs away in her red jumper before climbing into the red cab of Peter (Douglas Gordon), an apparently sympathetic truck driver. Red surrounds the duo at various points: red napkins when they eat, the red-and-white stripes of a windsock Peter gives Céline to play with, a cafe worker's red zipped sweater. Agnès B asks us to question their relationship based on the abusive one Céline has suffered up to this point. She warns us, and yet we mislead ourselves. Peter is not out to hurt Céline but to watch over her; the only person in danger of being hurt is him.

Fashion was not Agnès B's first career choice. Having produced nearly 30 films since the nineties, she has found her true creative outlet in cinema – she is a film-maker by choice, a designer by accident.

Despite the designer's involvement in the film, the red
Agnès B sweater worn by Lou-Lélia Demerliac in *My Name
is Hmmm...* was sourced from a flea market

ANDRÉ COURRÈGES

TWO FOR THE ROAD (1967)
LA PISCINE (1969)

André Courrèges in his workshop at his Basque country farm in 1978

—

p14 A simple black bikini by André Courrèges for Romy Schneider in *La Piscine*. This superficially straightforward design is indicative of Courrèges's minimalist approach to fashion

With no yearning for nostalgia, André Courrèges has only ever been about the modern. Having worked for ten years with master couturier and king of the ball gown Cristóbal Balenciaga, Courrèges is an expert cutter. This is echoed throughout all his collections, from 1961, when he established the Courrèges brand, to his groundbreaking 1964 'Moon Girl' collection, and beyond.

'Moon Girl' was one of the most significant collections of the sixties. Taking inspiration from the clean mod silhouettes of Swinging London, particularly those of designer John Bates, Courrèges created a stripped-down intergalactic utopia that would go on to be referenced for the rest of the decade. His slim pants, minidresses, miniskirts and A-line coats in clinical white and red were adorned with scalloped hems, patch pockets and gold buttons, accessorized with silk scarves, ribbed woollen tights and white kid boots. If Courrèges cannot individually lay claim to inventing the miniskirt – an honour he shares with Bates and fellow British designer Mary Quant – he did bring it to affluent Paris. Courrèges was one of a new breed of fresh creatives who personified possibly the most important period of fashion evolution in the twentieth century.

Courrèges's famous 'Eskimo' sunglasses, based on Inuit goggles, were first introduced in his 'Moon Girl' collection in 1965

Along with Mary Quant, Courrèges popularized the A-line shift dress during the 1960s. His clothes were designed to skim rather than hug the body

Courrèges was just one of the names Audrey Hepburn selected in her quest to appear young and relevant again in *Two for the Road* (1967; see also page 144). His contribution was scant but, as part of Hepburn's hip designer aesthetic, has stood the test of time. Hepburn plays Joanna, who begins the story an innocent girl next door, and ends it married, one affair down and draped head to toe in the latest space-age trends. *Two for the Road* has become one of the actress's most culturally relevant projects because it encapsulates a seismic shift in the fashion market that has remained in place ever since – essentially, the definitive arrival of youth. From the sixties onward, clothes would be for and about teenagers; fading adults like Hepburn, once darling fashionistas, would be reduced to playing catch-up. Courrèges provided a pair of white plastic wrap-around sunglasses for *Two for the Road* based on his own 'Eskimo' style, introduced in 1965, featuring mere slits for eyeholes. Hepburn's goggle versions in the movie are somewhat more user-friendly.

Courrèges was the sole credited costumier for *La Piscine* (*The Swimming Pool*, 1969). His looks for both female leads, Marianne (Romy Schneider) and

Penelope (Jane Birkin), are nothing less than a capsule retrospective of the designer's entire sixties back catalogue: everything from a dropped-waist flared shift with contrast piping, to a swirly print halter-maxi, to blue cigarette pants and upturned collar shirt, plus a sizeable quota of Courrèges's speciality, swimwear. *La Piscine* is set at a holiday villa in the South of France, which becomes a hub for sexual tension and jealousy in the searing Mediterranean heat. Penelope is a morose teenager dressed in young fashions such as jeans and shirts, with a childish gingham motif only adding to her perceived incorruptibility. Marianne is older and sharper, her style less mischievous. Both women wear swimwear in either black or white. For Marianne, this seems to reflect a sudden change in her personality; furious after being tossed into the pool by her boyfriend, she switches from a black bikini with gold aspect to a plain white one-piece and is suddenly calm and playful again. Their attire alludes to the lines Courrèges designed in the late sixties, in particular a white see-through shirt Penelope wears on arrival at the villa, without a bra, her nipples strate-gically covered by patch pockets. The clothes are not

Audrey Hepburn in *Two for the Road*, wearing wrap-around
shades by Courrèges, derived from his 'Eskimo' sunglasses

intended to accentuate a curvaceous female form, but rather to de-erotize a leaner, boyish physique. His designs are impish and fun, with any sexual connotations conferred only by us as spectators.

Costumier Michael Kaplan used reference books on André Courrèges as inspiration for *Star Trek: Into Darkness* (2013). Since J. J. Abrams's rebooted *Star Trek* films are in essence prequels to the television series that began in 1966, Kaplan wanted to remain grounded in that era's retro futurism. This brings costume in the franchise full circle, with the original show's clothing, such as A-line minidresses and body-hugging jersey shirts, a nod to the pioneering work of Courrèges.

André Courrèges has a tremendous legacy in film, if only a handful of direct appearances. Without his 'Moon Girl' collection it is debatable whether the celebrated costumes by Hardy Amies for *2001: A Space Odyssey* (1968) would have existed (see page 95). For the first time in history, fashion was led by the street. Courrèges, along with the likes of Paco Rabanne and Pierre Cardin, were taking trends like shapelessness and androgyny, and making them couture.

AZZEDINE ALAÏA

A VIEW TO A KILL (1985)
VAMP (1986)
GRAFFITI BRIDGE (1990)

Azzedine Alaïa in his workshop. As much a sculptor as a designer, Alaïa constructs garments, creates form

—

p20 This pseudo-masculine leather jacket paired with overtly feminine black heels is typical of the androgynous look that Alaïa designed for Grace Jones in *A View to a Kill*

Not a household name to the uninitiated but still remembered as a hugely important designer, Azzedine Alaïa – 'The King of Cling' – exemplified the eighties and nineties, his most prolific decades, with the close-fitting 'bodycon' look. Bodycon, short for 'body conscious', refers to a skin-tight garment that paradoxically is all about freeing the figure rather than restricting it. Alaïa makes significant use of Lycra to allow ease of movement and pull focus toward form. Not one to play by the rules, he releases collections according to his own timetable. Alaïa is a stubborn though well-liked and respected innovator, much like his muse – model, singer and actress Grace Jones.

Grace Jones personifies the Azzedine Alaïa woman. Powerful, athletic and angular, she even carried the petite Tunisian designer on stage to collect his award for Best Collection at the Oscars de la Mode in 1984. He dressed Jones on screen just twice: as super-buff villain May Day in the James Bond adventure *A View to a Kill* (1985) and as seductress Katrina in cult horror film *Vamp* (1986). It is Bond that everyone remembers most. Jones wears Alaïa's trademark cowls and hoods with such aplomb that separating actress and character is near on impossible. If Grace Jones ever turned to crime, she would be May Day.

Azzedine Alaïa sculpts the human body. Not all of his clothes are skintight, but all are designed to express fluidity of movement. Nowhere is this more evident than on Grace Jones in *A View to a Kill*. From a backless red dress with detachable hood and oversize black fez to extremely high-leg leotard and heelless buckled leg warmers, Jones's every costume has to accommodate the requirements of narrative, in this case taming a horse and teaching karate, regardless of how fantastical the overall aesthetic. Most of her ensembles are at least partly leather, the fabric that made Alaïa's name in the early eighties as his flared leather coats crept out of Paris on supermodel clients and onto the bustling New York fashion scene.

The most intriguing outfit Jones dons in *A View to a Kill* is her most rudimentary – a café-au-lait post-workout robe, backless with draped and folded neckline and one overhanging cap sleeve. It sums up how unable Azzedine Alaïa is to make anything 'ordinary' and how unwilling Jones would be to wear such an item. Jones sports a dozen costumes in the film, some amalgamations of each other. This is similar to Alaïa's design approach as a whole: many of his garments from the eighties especially are made up of several pieces joined together. Jones's studded leather jacket with lattice stitching and eaves shoulders worn over a black hood contrast-lined in yellow are clear examples of this concept. Incidentally, Alaïa was not solely responsible for creating Jones's ensembles. They were originally sketched by costumier Emma Porteous then made by the designer according to her specifications. Sadly, Porteous's name is often neglected in discussions of the film's costumes.

Grace Jones brought Azzedine Alaïa onboard for *Vamp*, along with some of her other creative friends, including activist and artist Keith Haring, fashion designer Issey Miyake, and even (at this juncture) photographer Andy Warhol. Little of their contribution is visible in the movie, except for Haring's striking 'flesh graffiti', which is probably down to their involvement being solely to placate Jones, whose presence was a real coup for producers of a low-budget teen horror flick. Jones's own minimal appearance is as ancient Egyptian vampire Katrina, awake and hungry in contemporary Los Angeles. A stripper in a dive nightclub, she lures men backstage for a 'bite'. Jones's big moment is a theatrical striptease in front of an open-mouthed crowd of drunks. Over skin covered in Haring's designs, Jones wears a long, willowy red jersey dress with angel sleeves and bodice that unzips to reveal a coiled silver wire bikini. Alaïa provided the slinky gown and Miyake, an expert in the innovative use of material and fabric, contributed her metalwork undergarments, a collaboration with jeweller David Spada. Later Jones wears a twisted aluminium headdress and corset, again almost certainly Miyake. Of all the creative input here, including that of costume designer Betty Pecha Madden, Alaïa knows the most about creating performance wear. Having made costumes for the prestigious Crazy Horse cabaret club in Paris, he appreciates that stage costume, particularly in the context of dancing and stripping, is as much about concealing the body as revealing it. Jones's barely seen finale dress, a white

p22 left Grace Jones in *A View to a Kill* wearing a skintight 'bodycon' garment that paradoxically frees her movement
—
p22 right Jones's Alaïa leather jacket with huge batwing sleeves, ideal for tossing henchman around without binding under the arm
—
p23 left Alaïa's ensembles in *Vamp* are largely concealed by darkness. This briefly seen garment, for example, is actually vivid red on screen
—
p23 right Jill Jones with Prince in *Graffiti Bridge*, Alaïa's last, and rather subdued, foray into costume design over a quarter of a century ago

bodycon turtleneck in chiffon silk, is just transparent enough to expose her spiral underwear before she is burned alive by sunlight.

With his last official screen credit for singer Jill Jones in Prince's *Graffiti Bridge* (1990), it is doubtful Azzedine Alaïa will make a return to film costuming. Alaïa's look is preserved, however, in Grace Jones as May Day in an industrial zipped batwing leather jacket and orange fabric-lined hood, lifting a grown man above her head – a glorious reminder of everything the designer stands for.

BERNARD NEWMAN

ROBERTA (1935)
TOP HAT (1935)
SWING TIME (1936)
THEODORA GOES WILD (1936)

Bernard Newman (seated at front left) and designers
Orry-Kelly, Travis Banton, Edith Head, and Irene at the
Los Angeles Fashion Futures Show, 1941
—
p24 Ginger Rogers in a dress designed by Bernard
Newman for *Swing Time*. Tiny lead weights in the hem
ensured the dress swung in a satisfying circular motion

Even though he never really left the fashion
industry, Bernard Newman's short-lived tenure
as a costume designer has come to define his
career. He created stunning gowns in the thirties
born of Hollywood's reaction to the Great Depression,
giving cinemagoers the glamour they craved.

After working his way up to chief designer
at department store Bergdorf Goodman in New York,
Newman spent 12 years there before leaving for
Hollywood in 1933. He spent three years making
garments for more than 20 films starring, among
others, Irene Dunne, Lucille Ball and, his favourite,
Ginger Rogers. Initially under contract to RKO Pictures,
then freelance, Newman worked for Columbia Pictures
and Warner Bros. well into the forties. An exacting
though generous man, Newman recommended that
costumier Edward Stevenson, whom he had worked
alongside, take over at RKO after he left.

Despite arriving in Hollywood two years before,
Newman's first credited project was *Roberta* (1935).
Irene Dunne starred as Stephanie, loyal assistant at
Paris fashion house Roberta, and Ginger Rogers played
Lizzie Gatz, an American masquerading as Polish
entertainer 'Countess Scharwenka'. The budget was a
rumoured quarter of a million dollars, plenty of which
was lavished on the costume design, especially during

the last-act fashion show in which ensemble after ensemble is paraded as if in an extended commercial. Supposedly as many as fifteen costumes from the film were recreated by the Modern Merchandising Bureau. The bureau was Hollywood's attempt to stop their designs being blatantly copied by department stores. These recreated and 'inspired by' dresses were sold through Cinema Fashion Shops. The shops sold only women's clothing; no garments were recreated from men's costumes as male actors generally provided their own attire, unless the film was a period production.

In *Roberta*, Stephanie takes over at the fashion house and attempts to breathe fresh life into the classic brand with new designs. This gave Newman the opportunity to let loose with some outlandish creations, one of which – a long-sleeve sheath, seemingly constructed of black latex (really only used for swimsuits at this time) with a huge bow to the shoulder, worn by Stephanie – seems just as bizarre today. Rogers gets the lion's share of luxurious costumes. Her choicest ensemble is not a dress but an oddly structured jumpsuit with black silk velvet flared trousers that rise past the natural waistline, meeting a cropped waistcoat attached to a shirt with gathered sleeves and a bow tie. It appears to be an all-in-one garment, though designed to resemble a two-piece dinner suit with separate shirt (she later adds a matching tuxedo jacket), a daring look that Marlene Dietrich had brought into the public consciousness in *Morocco* (1930). The gold lamé dress, however, is Rogers's own garment, a Newman design that the actress had purchased before even starting the film.

Some of the 'fashionable' gowns in *Roberta* will seem peculiar, even amusing, to contemporary eyes. The fashion show sequence is a technical feat for Newman. There does not seem to be a great deal of cohesion between the outfits twirled in front of eyes, though some of the creations – namely, a staggering fur number worn by Lucille Ball – are memorable flights of fancy. Yes, *Roberta* is dated, but surely any film set in the world of fashion by very definition should be?

Newman worked with Ginger Rogers on *Top Hat* (1935) to create one notorious costume in particular: the 'feather dress' worn during her 'Cheek to Cheek' routine with Fred Astaire. Pale blue in a bias cut with an on-trend revealing low back, it is a classic addition to Newman's CV, though it would surely not be so well remembered without the ostrich feathers Rogers insisted be added. As Rogers and Astaire danced, feathers shed everywhere, enough even to be picked up by the camera.

In *Swing Time* (1936), Newman exhibits more variety in costume than a typically glossy Fred and Ginger picture. Their characters in the film are quite ordinary: Fred Astaire plays John, a jobbing dancer, and Ginger Rogers a dance school instructor, Penny. In keeping with the characters, Newman dials down the glitz a notch – just a notch, mind. Rogers still gets

p26 top This dress designed by Newman, with input from star Ginger Rogers, for *Top Hat* is perhaps the designer's best remembered work
—
p26 bottom Ginger Rogers takes centre stage in the *Roberta* fashion show, though this is actually one of Newman's more restrained outfits
—
p27 Irene Dunne in *Theodora Goes Wild*, wearing a Bernard Newman coat trimmed in real gorilla fur – amazingly, not a controversial fabric choice in the 1930s

the fancy gowns, with one in particular comparable to *Top Hat*'s feather dress in terms of lavishness, but also pared-down daywear that is arguably just as elegant. The black dress Penny wears during the 'Pick Yourself Up' waltz, with its pleated skirt, fitted bodice, Peter Pan neckline and gently rolled shoulder, harks back to twenties sportswear. Later, for the 'Never Gonna Dance' sequence, Rogers dons her most dramatic costume, again co-designed with Newman: a light pink silk georgette bias-cut evening gown in two layers of fabric, with French seams and cape that extends across her back and arms like bat wings. As with the 'Pick Yourself Up' dress, tiny weights were sewn into the hem to give the skirt requisite swish as Rogers danced.

Infamous today for one outrageous costume, *Theodora Goes Wild* (1936) is nonetheless an excellent showcase for Newman's grasp of the methodology of costume design and how it can be employed to help tell a story. Irene Dunne is Theodora, prim Sunday school teacher and secret writer of scandalous literature. Newman costumes Theodora as a split personality; her day-to-day existence is actually a disguise. Theodora wears tea dresses with Peter Pan collars and puff sleeves, their prints, a mixture of floral and geometric, the only hint of anything lurking beneath the facade. Prints in vivid Cubist or Art Deco patterns were exceptionally popular during the thirties, either as trim or covering entire dresses and blouses. When

Theodora finally discards her repressed self, the first outfit she wears causes open mouths all around. Marching into her publisher's office wrapped in a genuine gorilla fur coat and matching hat, the subtext is difficult to ignore. This is Theodora 'going wild' like an ape. The costume itself would have been shocking in the thirties simply due to its extravagance, but now can only be seen as vulgar, even offensive. From this point on in the story, Theodora is attired in only the most glittering of outfits, most of which are trimmed in fur. One ensemble, however, is a shocking, deeply unflattering disaster – a dark lamé coat with high upturned collar and bow worn over matching slim-leg trousers. It is a costume in every sense of the word, for both Dunne and Theodora, implying that perhaps Theodora has gone a little *too* wild.

Newman's work in *Theodora Goes Wild* demonstrates that he well understood the difference between his work at Bergdorf's and his work in cinema: what we see in the movies, alluring or otherwise, is not necessarily designed to be worn in real life. His finest work on screen is resolutely designed to stay there.

BILL BLASS

ADVISE AND CONSENT (1962)
THE DEVIL WEARS PRADA (2006)
THE BUTLER (2013)

Bill Blass in 1977. Blass was an ambassador for his brand:
well groomed and charming at all the right parties

—

p28 Meryl Streep wearing a deliberately loud bead-detail
gold jacket by Bill Blass for *The Devil Wears Prada*

You want to drive American, you buy Ford; you want to dress American, you buy Bill Blass. In the TV series *Fargo* (2014–) reborn doormat Lester Nygaard (Martin Freeman) upgrades his life with a new job, house, wife, car and clothes. 'Bill Blass,' he says proudly of his new black single-breasted suit. To Americans, especially those who have worn a blue collar, Bill Blass is a name that it is legitimately okay to spend your money on. Nothing froufrou about this designer; those who wear Blass on screen are can-do people and unashamed flag wavers.

Bill Blass was a practical man with a sharp eye for simple yet provocative style, on others and himself. He launched his menswear line in 1967 and was his own best advertisement; men bought Blass suits because they wanted to look like Blass himself. Blass did not have a signature style as such, mainly because he was not an artist. Clothes to Blass were to wear, not hang in gallery installations. During the seventies in particular he was a known socialite; he was less about making fashion than living the scene itself. His dresses were made to inflame without setting the room on fire. First Lady Nancy Reagan was a lifelong fan, as were Jacqueline Kennedy and Barbara Bush, which really tells us all we need to know. Bill Blass ladies have grace, aplomb and plenty of cash, but are never vulgar.

Director Otto Preminger tempted actress Gene Tierney out of retirement for *Advise and Consent* (1962) on the promise that Bill Blass would design her costumes. Blass had obvious appeal to an old-school star like Tierney; he would make her look incredible but not showy. Her return to film would be a 'wow' moment rather than a 'whoa'. *Advise and Consent* is a cracking political thriller. Although Tierney barely features, her role as legislator's wife Dolly Harrison is made unquestionably more memorable by the clothes she wears. Most important of all, Blass's costumes are entirely suitable for her character. Dolly has a professional, stately presence and knows how to make everyone happy; she is the type of woman who understands exactly what works on her figure. Dolly's main Blass ensemble is worn for an evening soirée when she must glide from guest to guest being charming and elegant, yet unthreatening to the beady gaze of fellow wives. She wears a full-length sleeveless black dress in silk chiffon with high neckline, sheer back and décolletage, silver brooch underneath the bust and a long matching train attached like a scarf, which she holds in her arm in the same way a label-obsessed fashionista today would flaunt a statement handbag. However, there is no display here; Dolly is all about meticulous modesty. It is easy to see how Bill Blass came to be credited as reviving the cocktail dress during the seventies. His

talent for eveningwear, especially for – to observe the morality of the period – married women, was unparalleled. Dolly's black dress is the kind of garment Betty Draper in the television series *Mad Men* (2007–15) would have worn. That Bill Blass is best remembered for dressing the wives of prominent men does not mean his customer base was meek or subservient, just that they comprehended the conventions of their time.

Costume designer Patricia Field chose several Bill Blass items for tyrannical magazine editor Miranda Priestly (Meryl Streep) in *The Devil Wears Prada* (2006). Her twinkly gold jacket (Michael Vollbracht for Bill Blass), cut along the lines of a classic Chanel box suit of the fifties, is rich boss attire. Miranda owns everyone in a room; Blass reminds people of that fact without Miranda having to open her mouth. She also wears a Bill Blass black shirt/jacket, black dress, plush Nouveau pattern jacket and assorted blouses. Blass is a look that can be dressed up or down, depending on the occasion. In cinema it represents glitzy allure, but only on confident women assured of who they are.

Costumier Ruth Carter did not have the budget to go full designer for the extravagant gowns required in *The Butler* (2013). Since much of the story is set in and around the White House, incorporating several real-life characters, this was a tough sell. Carter recreated items herself, inspired by era-specific labels. However,

Jane Fonda, playing Nancy Reagan, wanted only genuine Bill Blass and James Galanos. Blass was friends
with Nancy Reagan and, as such, was invited to all
the high-profile parties. He barely spoke about fashion,
which is probably what made him such a popular guest.
Nancy Reagan was the Bill Blass customer personified.
She knew how to make an entrance but never toyed
with impropriety. For *The Butler*, Fonda wore a red-and-
black dress with floor-length skirt, seen on Reagan
during Christmas celebrations in 1983. It is indicative
of the period, but stops short of datable details.

Bill Blass was his brand, and although it
continued after his retirement in 1999, something of
the magic went with him. Thanks to television and
film, though, the archetypal Blass man and woman will
always be remembered in their prime.

BROOKS BROTHERS

THE ADJUSTMENT BUREAU (2011)
ARGO (2012)
THE GREAT GATSBY (2013)

Catherine Martin, costume designer for the movie *The Great Gatsby* looks at original costume sketches, 2013

—

p32 Leonardo DiCaprio in *The Great Gatsby* wearing a pink suit made by Brooks Brothers, finished in linen and featuring turnback 'gauntlet' cuffs

It is hardly surprising that Brooks Brothers appears all over the world of film and television as it is the oldest retail establishment in the United States. Founded in 1818 by Henry S. Brooks, the company has come to define the distinguished American man. Presidents, sports stars, captains of industry, and screen characters ranging from mysterious millionaire Jay Gatsby to suave Madison Avenue ad man Don Draper all sum up the appeal of a Brooks Brothers suit: legacy.

Cinema's ongoing relationship with Brooks Brothers is only possible because of the company's heritage: the organization was family run for 128 years before being sold to Julius Garfinckel and Co.; it is now owned by Brooks Brothers Incorporated. Ideally placed to provide for an industry that requires speedy turnaround, it can offer costume designers a vast archive of period styles and fabrics. Catherine Martin, producer, set designer and costumier for *The Great Gatsby* (2013), chose to work with Brooks Brothers for this very reason, plus the fact that *Gatsby*'s author F. Scott Fitzgerald had referred to the company by name several times in his text. Fitzgerald's anti-hero Jay Gatsby (played in this version by Leonardo DiCaprio; see page 174 for Robert Redford's turn in the role) is a self-made man. Staggeringly rich but without a past,

he needs Brooks Brothers to provide an air of legitimacy – a heritage of his own. Martin and director Baz Luhrmann approached their version of the classic novel with an eye to period accuracy but set across an entire decade – the enormously changeable silhouette of the twenties. The Brooks Brothers suits worn by DiCaprio and co-star Tobey Maguire, who plays Yale graduate Nick Carraway, are a fitted early-twenties cut that is more flattering to modern eyes than the wider proportions seen in the latter part of the decade. Brooks Brothers employed master tailor Martin Greenfield, at this point in his early eighties, to coordinate production of all DiCaprio and Maguire's suits. In total the company supplied 500 ensembles for the cast and extras, made up of 1,700 pieces, including shoes, ties and shirts.

Tailor Martin Greenfield is well known in the film and television industry. He has collaborated with Brooks Brothers several times, as well as personally creating suits for productions such as *The Wolf of Wall Street* (2013), *Boardwalk Empire* (2010–14) and *The Knick* (2014–). The suits worn by DiCaprio and Maguire in *The Great Gatsby* were researched by Catherine Martin and then made by Greenfield and his team. Catherine Martin was keen to ensure that everything had precedent in real life. The dapper pink pinstriped suit worn

by Gatsby on his trip to New York's Plaza Hotel with Daisy was a piece viewers expected to see in the movie, especially after Robert Redford wore a comparable example in his incarnation of Gatsby in 1974. Martin managed to confirm its existence by combing through Brooks Brothers' archive. She discovered the brand had been making these suits in seersucker since the late nineteenth century – to all intents and purposes the first versions in the United States. Even though Brooks Brothers is a patriotic US establishment, its silhouette – what we now describe as a lounge suit of single-breasted suit jacket and matching trousers – was keenly influenced by late-Victorian-era Savile Row. Likewise, the button-down shirt that Brooks Brothers profess to have invented was based on an English polo shirt with buttons fastened to the collars to hold them in place during play. The 'sack suit', a roomy-fitting style made with no darts and two stitched panels to the rear of the jacket, is more an American convention than anything else – just the type of suit Brooks Brothers are best known for tailoring. Nonetheless, this is exactly the opposite of the style they produced under Catherine Martin's guidance for *The Great Gatsby*.

The benefits of Brooks Brothers' past collections are obvious for costume designers hoping to reproduce specific items on film. For the political

thriller *Argo* (2012), costumier Jacqueline West asked Brooks Brothers, via Martin Greenfield, to copy the suits worn by real-life CIA agent Tony Mendez (played by Ben Affleck), sometimes mixed as separates, sometimes as sports jackets and jeans.

For science-fiction romance *The Adjustment Bureau* (2011), costume designer Kasia Walicka-Maimone was more interested in what the brand said as an embodiment of timeless style when selecting the smart uniform suits and raincoats sported by the movie's antagonists, aka The Bureau.

In recent years, Brooks Brothers have been part of numerous retail tie-ins, namely *Mad Men* costumier Janie Bryant's limited-edition sharkskin suit and separates collection, and their 'Great Gatsby' range, which included tipped blazers and pink linen trousers. Such deals extend the life of clothing by capitalizing upon their movie associations as a unique selling point – youthful preppiness for *Gatsby*, and enduring sixties and seventies cool for *Mad Men* – bringing Brooks Brothers' immense heritage to life via period interpretations both in cinemas and on the street. They even received a backhanded namecheck in sci-fi thriller *Tenet* (2020). For a film about time, it makes sense to reference a brand as timeless as the suit itself.

CALVIN KLEIN

PLAYERS (1979)
CLUELESS (1995)
THE DEVIL WEARS PRADA (2006)

Calvin Klein in his workroom in New York City, 1985
—
p36 Ali MacGraw and Dean-Paul Martin in *Players*. Even though Calvin Klein designed all of MacGraw's costumes, the film remains little seen

For those who were teenagers during the eighties or nineties, Calvin Klein is more about underwear than anything else. Indeed this idea even accounts for a clever visual quip in *Back to the Future* (1985), when it is assumed to be Marty McFly's (Michael J. Fox) name because the logo is stitched on his briefs. Having that clean, understated Calvin Klein label popping above denim jeans slung low on the hips was a style imperative. Calvin Klein might be minimal, but thanks to extensive advertising, licensing and name-checking in one of the most influential teen fashion movies of all time, the brand itself is far from inconspicuous.

Calvin Klein is all easy. Since its inception by New Yorker Klein in 1968, originally for coats and sportswear, the brand has followed a manifesto of comfortable, simple style. Appropriately, Klein made his name with high-waist denim jeans in the early seventies, his name tag sewn on the seat for all to see. Calvin Klein continues an American trend for revamping sports and leisure garments as everyday apparel for life and work. Claire McCardell was the instigator of this innovation in the forties, employing fabrics such as cotton gingham, calico, even denim. Movie costumiers tend to use Calvin Klein as a symbol of youth (or the appearance of) and the informal charm of ingrained American self-confidence. Klein only has one cinematic

wardrobe credit to his name, for Ali MacGraw in forgotten romantic drama *Players* (1979). This is a pity
because the Calvin Klein look has probably never been
sold so convincingly, on screen or off.

In *Players*, Ali MacGraw is Nicole, an older
woman of means who begins a relationship with a
younger man, tennis ace Chris (Dean-Paul Martin).
Nicole's style is spare minimalist, monotone biscuit
shades in fabrics so light they waft constantly in the
breeze. Her wardrobe is a uniform mix, perceptibly by
one designer, of shirt dresses, knitted jersey dresses,
long slightly flared skirts, revere collar shirts and white
denim jeans. Even though Nicole's overall look is near
distractingly ahead of its time, the ensembles themselves are simplicity personified. On her first evening
with Chris she wears only a beige just-below-the-knee
skirt and black long sleeve sweater tucked in, accessorized with two silver cuffs. Her hurriedly put together
travelling outfit consists of a loose-fitting grey trench-
coat and white crew-neck tee. Casual day attire is a
generally a check shirt and white jeans or skirt. Every
shirt either has the sleeves rolled up or turned back and
is knotted at the front, buttons open just enough to give
the impression of being thrown on. This sexy, hastily
fastened style would soon be mimicked by Brooke
Shields in her controversial Calvin Klein jeans ads –
controversial because she was only fifteen at the time.
Nicole's silhouette is not masculine but unisex, a notion
Klein revisited with his CK One fragrance for both men
and women in 1994. The effortlessness of MacGraw's
clothing intensifies her beauty. Klein kept Nicole's attire
so uniform, seemingly so unthinking, that it reflects
precisely who she is. Nicole is not constrained by any
suggestion that feminine must mean 'girly'. Even a
white off-the-shoulder gypsy dress worn for her birth-
day party is unadorned to the degree that it appears to
have been slipped it on mere seconds before arriving.
Ali MacGraw in *Players* is everything it means to choose
Calvin Klein: laid-back, elegant cool.

From hardly seen to iconic, Calvin Klein's most
famous appearance in cinema was a defining moment
in high-school-set comedy *Clueless* (1995). Costume
designer Mona May created a new trend for the rich
kids of Beverly Hills. Youths in uptown Los Angeles were
experimenting with urban grunge, but May felt a more
optimistic, colourful, slightly fantastical palette would
be more in keeping with the story. Throughout the film,
beaming all-American girl Cher (Alicia Silverstone)
sports wild tartan miniskirts, preppy shirts, and over-
the-knee socks – not the Calvin Klein look in any way
shape or form. This is precisely why when Cher dons a
white Calvin Klein stretch cotton shift for an important
date: it has such an impact. Despite the dress being
virtuous white, its fit, which does seem to be one size
too small, is contoured to reveal every curve of Cher's
still developing figure. She is a confident yet naive
teenager in a woman's body. Klein has actually been

associated with this kind of controversy before. His highly sexualized ads featuring the adolescent Shields, for example, and later model Kate Moss who was only seventeen when draped half naked across then pop star Mark Wahlberg, plus many more instances since. Nonetheless, in the context of *Clueless* what this ensemble says about Cher is that she's growing up. Of course, what makes the reveal even more memorable is the amusing exchange Cher has with her father: 'What's that?' 'A dress.' 'Says who?' 'Calvin Klein.' The costume remains so well loved that in 2010, Hollywood boutique Confederacy persuaded Calvin Klein to re-release the exact style dress (in red too) for a limited run in their stores. With the nineties now termed 'vintage' in fashion, this dress has become a seminal garment from the era.

The fist-pumping all-American girl wearing Calvin Klein is a concept also used for *The Devil Wears Prada* (2006). Costumier Patricia Field selected a cotton jersey dress by the brand for aspirant journo Andrea Sachs (Anne Hathaway). Most of Hathaway's ensembles are Chanel. They are luscious, though rigidly fitted and not suitable for more than tapping keys at a desk or delivering no-fat lattes. Field chose the Calvin Klein dress as a notable exception because, being worn across several scenes, it needed to be non-intrusive to the audience and comfortable for the actress to wear. Costume has to be considered in context, but also from a practical perspective. None of the scenes could be 'about' Andrea's dress; it did not have a narrative role to play. Klein can do showstopper, yet will always function best as a practical alternative to the artistic whims of more extravagant designers.

p38 top Before becoming an actress, Ali MacGraw was a fashion model, through which she developed a working relationship with Calvin Klein, who dressed her on screen for *Players*. Here she wears a typically unisex styled Calvin Klein silk shirt

—

p38 bottom Alicia Silverstone in the famous Calvin Klein *Clueless* dress, worn with a see-through shirt

—

p39 Anne Hathaway in a green jersey dress provided by Calvin Klein for *The Devil Wears Prada*. Costumier Patricia added the leather belt for understated visual interest

CECIL BEATON

GIGI (1958)

MY FAIR LADY (1964)

ON A CLEAR DAY YOU CAN SEE FOREVER (1970)

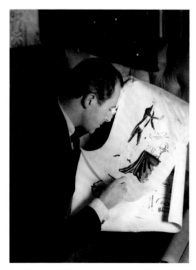

Cecil Beaton at work on costume designs, 1940
—
p40 Cecil Beaton created all of Barbra Streisand's costumes for the period flashbacks in *On a Clear Day You Can See Forever*, though many of his creations were cut from the final film

Sir Cecil Beaton is known primarily as a photographer; yet he was also a respected painter, actor, fashion designer and costumier.

You were not really anyone, especially from the thirties onward when he moved to Hollywood, unless Cecil Beaton took your picture. Beaton's approach was to make everything perfect. Were he alive today, Beaton the photographer would likely have been a big fan of Photoshop. His photographs of the twentieth century's most famous faces were always flattering; many of his images were published in *Vogue* magazine, and he was officially commissioned to take portraits of the British Royal Family. Beaton was ambitious and forever striving. After conquering one industry, he would actively seek to reign in another. This quest for perfection led to costume designing for the stage and screen. His first foray into the world of costume was designing outfits for charity matinées (he designed book jackets too). However, Beaton did not create for film until after World War II. Costume seemingly came as easy to Beaton as everything else he attempted; two of his films went on to win Academy Awards for costume design in *Gigi* (1958) and *My Fair Lady* (1964).

Beaton was the costumier for the 1956 Broadway production of *My Fair Lady*, and his vision for director George Cukor's film version, starring Audrey

Hepburn as Eliza Doolittle and Rex Harrison as Professor Henry Higgins, retained the hyper-Edwardian aesthetic Beaton had developed for the stage. Beaton was also art director on the film, which was highly unusual, even though, given Beaton's skill set, it made perfect sense. Eliza is a transformation role, a drab flower girl who becomes a society darling adorned in a wardrobe so extravagant it almost segues into fantasy. Beaton's period recreations were accurate in terms of shape and overall style, with embellishments made to augment the unbridled luxury. His faithful eye extended beyond Eliza too; Rex Harrison wears era-correct black patent leather dress pumps (like slippers) with silk bows to complete his splendid white-tie evening ensemble.

My Fair Lady's Royal Ascot scene encapsulates the sheer lavishness of the film. Not only was Audrey Hepburn garbed in an incredible dress, hat and parasol, but each of the 400 other characters featured in the scene was dressed in a gown specially designed for the actress wearing it. These were not 'extras' or extras' costumes; Beaton knew Hepburn was the star, but these women all had to shine individually. Beaton loosely based his costumes on the infamous 'Black Ascot' of 1910, where patrons were instructed to wear black to acknowledge the death of King Edward VII. Although Beaton departs from historical representation in terms of colour, sticking to a palette of mainly white, black and medium grey, his dress forms remain the same. There was little concession made to 'toning down' the silhouette in 1910. For many, Hepburn's dress in My Fair Lady symbolizes what film costume is all about: grandiosity you could never actually wear in real life. The Ascot scene undoubtedly went a long way to securing Beaton's Academy Award for costume design (he also won for art direction) – with Hepburn's gown close to winning it single-handedly. There might be no more ornately glamorous costume in cinema history. The ensemble comprised silk linen underclothes, overlaid with fine lace and hand-embroidered flower motif; dress trimmed in black-and-white-striped velvet ribbon with a large bow to the left breast; and wide-brim hat in cotton burlap, trimmed in black-and-white-striped velvet and topped with ostrich feathers and faux pansies. Without question, it announces Eliza's arrival as a 'lady', even as it mummified Hepburn's narrow frame in a rigid Edwardian silhouette that no more encouraged sitting down than it did eating a healthy lunch. In actuality, no one could wear this dress and function, but that is irrelevant. It is emblematic, both in narrative context and as a symbol for Hollywood itself – the ultimate escape from reality.

Another of Beaton's best-known costuming achievements is the period/fantasy segments of On a Clear Day You Can See Forever (1970). Arnold Scaasi designed Barbra Streisand's (very) contemporary costumes as kooky Daisy Gamble, with Beaton throwing everything he could at what came to be scant minutes

p42 top Actress Leslie Caron and Cecil Beaton on the set of *Gigi*

—

p42 bottom Audrey Hepburn as Eliza Doolittle in *My Fair Lady*, dressed for the races at Ascot in Cecil Beaton's best-known creation for the screen

—

p43 Cecil Beaton's sketch of Royal Ascot costumes for *My Fair Lady*. Beaton was also art director and set designer for the film – as such, he had a big hand in the production's entire look

of flashback screen-time. Beaton considered Streisand to be one of the most beautiful women in the world; Streisand was immensely flattered that he loved the bump in her famous nose. That said, Beaton's most accomplished dress for the film, certainly in terms of detailing, made a concerted effort to draw attention away from it. Her pearl-encrusted turban was supposed to be accessorized with a diamond nose stud, though Beaton advised against it. The dress is a white empire-line gown in crepe silk festooned with appliqué and silver embroidery. An empire line raises the natural waistline of a dress to just beneath the wearer's bust and can be flattering to a fuller figure or larger décolletage. Streisand liked the style because it left her diaphragm unconstrained for singing. Even without a diamond nose stud, the turban elongates Streisand's contours in the most attractive way, giving her a profile akin to ancient Egyptian beauty Nefertiti. Beaton was dismayed that many of his costumes were cut from the film due to issues with the script. Discovering unseen images of these rare ensembles has become something of a mission for Beaton and Streisand fans alike.

Cecil Beaton could not ever really be termed a fashion designer, but he did make clothes for photoshoots, such as dresses and miniskirts. Moreover, he was an incredibly dapper man himself, added to The Best Dressed List in 1970. Fashion ran through his veins, and he would likely have conquered that entire industry, at least for a time, had he not been busy conquering every other.

CHRISTIAN DIOR

STAGE FRIGHT (1950)
ARABESQUE (1966)

Christian Dior at work in his office, 1947. Although his life was cut short at just 52, the Dior name lives on as one of the most recognizable in fashion

—

p44 Marlene Dietrich in Christian Dior for Alfred Hitchcock's *Stage Fright*. The actress reputedly insisted on Dior providing her clothes before taking the role

Even those unfamiliar with the nuances of fashion know what Dior stands for: opulence. Christian Dior officially arrived in 1947 with his 'Carolle' collection, in which he introduced the New Look, accentuating bust, hips and narrow waist. This signature silhouette was a direct response to years of wartime uniforms and suits – cut like sacks, unadorned and purely functional – and would carry thorough to the fifties. Once again Paris ruled. Dior rebuilt the female figure with underdresses and boning, topped with yards of the finest fabric. This was not comfortable attire; the comfort in Dior's clothes came from knowing you looked amazing. Movie stars of the era were enraptured. Dior's reign in fashion lasted until his untimely death in 1957.

Marlene Dietrich modelled for Dior; they were friends, and he created the costumes for many of her later movies. She even purchased bespoke men's clothing for herself from the designer. Other major names associated with the house included Jayne Mansfield, Olivia de Havilland and Rita Hayworth, who chose a Dior gown for the premiere of *Gilda* (1946). Dior's connection with the arts extended to theatre and ballet; his 1947 collection was in part inspired by expansive ballerina skirts.

The tiny nipped-in waist of Dior's 1947 'New Look' heralded a return to feminine shapes after the stale uniformity of World War II

Autumn/Winter 2015 Dior ready-to-wear show, Tokyo, featuring a silhouette and materials that echo Sophia Loren's Bohan at Dior look for *Arabesque*

Dietrich's outfits as femme fatale Charlotte Inwood in Alfred Hitchcock's *Stage Fright* (1950) are a world away from the actress's quasi-masculine look. A waning star of the London stage, Charlotte is also a coolly composed suspected murderer. As with all femme fatales, her appearance is controlled and disproportionately prioritized. Most of her Dior ensembles are costumes within a costume. When performing or meeting her public, Charlotte's gowns are extravagant, festooned with ornate petals or trimmed in an abundance of feathers and often sit off the shoulder with a deep neckline. The garments craft a frame around her face, focusing attention on both the character and the actress. Off stage, Charlotte's Dior silhouette is more Digby Morton–inspired: tailored and flawless rather than ostentatious. Adornment is reserved for the glitzy Cartier jewellery Dietrich flashes, or a disconcertingly lifelike (it has a face) white fox fur stole.

Dietrich's first costume, a lightweight mushroom pleated silk gown, gently padded in the shoulders, with voluminous sleeves draped just beneath the elbow, is smeared with blood. In contrast to a classic femme fatale, Charlotte's perfect facade is immediately besmirched. The dress is so flimsy it can be scrunched up by Charlotte's lover and hidden under his suit in plain view of the police. Dior's creation is costume first – vital to the narrative – and fashion second. The distributors of *Stage Fright* were only too happy to use Dior's name in the film's marketing. His most elaborate creations, including a pink dress, again heavily pleated and gathered under the bust to form a characteristically complex Dior bodice, helped sell this unglamorous thriller to a wider audience. Fashion as costume was gathering momentum.

The period following *Stage Fright* was busy for Dior, including gowns for Myrna Loy as Mrs Cartwright in *The Ambassador's Daughter* (1956) and 14 separate costumes for Ava Gardner as Lady Susan Ashlow in *The Little Hut* (1957). When Christian Dior passed away of a heart attack in 1957, Yves Saint Laurent took over. Then with Marc Bohan in 1961 the house began its most successful period since the reign of Dior himself. Bolstered by a recent Nile cruise, Bohan came aboard with a lust for anything Middle Eastern. He incorporated these into stunning collections that, despite being ultramodern in scope, still managed to reference the house's New Look heyday.

The poster for *Arabesque* sports the subtitle 'So Mod!'
This PVC raincoat by Dior is probably the closest it comes
to fulfilling the statement

Arabesque (1966), a Stanley Donan production in the style of his biggest hit *Charade* (1963), is a spy adventure with expensive cars and sets and Sophia Loren's wardrobe exclusively designed by Bohan at Dior. The look is a mix of Asian exotica incorporating striking colours, prints and fabrics. A leopard-fur cloche with feathered dresses and slippers is combined with contemporary mod: long white PVC boots, bright-red PVC coat and white round-rimmed plastic sunglasses. Loren's exceedingly chic spy Yasmin Azir wears a fresh outfit for each scene. She greets her bumbling house-guest Professor Pollock (Gregory Peck) in a black dress (which he refers to as 'a nightie'), changes into a gold lamé gown with jewel-embellished hood to eat dinner, then later pops on a grey zebra-print dress, accessorized with a pink towel wrapped around her head, just to walk from bedroom to bathroom. Even in Yasmin's cover as a wealthy lady of leisure, these changes make little sense. However, like most of Donan's films, the story takes place in a heightened reality. *Arabesque* was a glamorous respite from the increasingly gritty and 'real' British 'kitchen sink' dramas of the era.

It takes a commanding presence like Loren to remain prioritized on the screen over her grandiose costumes. Her Races Day ensemble of white silk brocade dress and white wide-brim hat, both trimmed in white feathers, is amusingly extravagant, yet Loren wears it as effortlessly as a dressing gown. Her contract specified that she be allowed to keep all the specially made outfits after shooting. She had a private Dior collection entirely to herself.

Dior has such prominence in fashion history that costume designer Jacqueline Durran referenced its 'New Look' silhouette for *Anna Karenina* (2012), despite the film's being set in late-nineteenth-century Russia. She felt Dior's glamour – Hollywood's glamour, essentially – fit director Joe Wright's stylized and stagey adaptation, with clothes representing the era's unbending yet oddly alluring conformity. Raf Simons became creative director of Dior in 2012 and stayed for three years; his feature documentary *Dior and I* (2014) charts Christian Dior's journey to present his first collection, thus ensuring the Dior name continued its lifelong association with cinema.

COCO CHANEL

TONIGHT OR NEVER (1931)
LA RÈGLE DU JEU (1939)

Coco Chanel in 1936. Chanel kickstarted a revolution in women's fashion: comfort was deemed as important as display
—
p48 Gloria Swanson wearing a Chanel creation for *Tonight or Never*, only her second foray into Hollywood costume design

Born in France, 1883, Gabrielle 'Coco' Chanel was a milliner before she became a fashion designer. As her name took off, Chanel moved into designing clothes, founding her own house in 1909. A radical couturière, she wanted to free the constricted Belle Époque female form. Chanel used innovative fabrics like jersey knit wool, previously associated only with male underwear. Much of her philosophy came from the blending of gender boundaries, challenging acceptable norms. Women have Chanel to thank for popularizing trousers, collarless box suits and, eventually, the immortal little black dress. She changed everything.

After 1910, Chanel began designing for ballet, theatre and the screen. She ran with an arty set – though not so much as sworn rival Elsa Schiaparelli (see page 64) – including such luminaries as Jean Cocteau, mainly providing costumes for their pet projects. When Chanel retired from fashion in 1938 she also retired from movies, though she returned triumphantly with her restyled box suit in 1954. This bouclé suit was a revelation: a straight-cut jacket, no interfacing, chains sewn into the lining so it hung level, and functioning buttons, paired with an unadorned knee-length skirt; it gave Chanel a second being. Subsequently she continued to provide costumes for French cinema until the sixties. One of her best-known titles is

La Règle du Jeu (*The Rules of the Game*, 1939) for director Jean Renoir.

A commercial and critical disaster on its original release, *La Règle du Jeu* is now considered one of the best films ever made. In a decadent France on the eve of World War II, this cutting view of a morally defunct upper-class society hit too close to home for many. In 1939 Chanel revealed her final pre-War collection called 'Tricolor', a celebration of historical nationalism. It was one of her most exciting collections, though bears little relation to the costumes she provided for the principals of *La Règle du Jeu*. As expected among the rich, there is a lot of fur. Christine (Nora Gregor) arrives at the stately home where much of the story takes place in a genuine cheetah-fur coat and matching hat. With Chanel, however, even the extravagant is practical in some respects: as Christine removes the coat, she takes the unattached leather belt and fastens it around her straight-line jersey skirt. But for all the apparent sophistication of fur, Chanel's most elegant outfit for the film is Christine's hunting ensemble. Constructed of precisely tailored check tweed, the jacket is closely based on the Victorian male version, except it falls on the natural waist and is fitted closer to the body in a low double-breasted style. To the rear is a centre inverted pleat and two bi-swing pleats to allow ease of movement while shooting a rifle; the leather patch on her right shoulder is there to rest the butt on. Contrast this functional attire with the silk

night robe Christine wears later on, its huge bishop sleeves covered in white winter ermine fur. Chanel's costumes in *La Règle du Jeu* marry two worlds – the ornate and the functional – encapsulating her groundbreaking approach to women's fashion.

In 1931 Chanel worked for a brief period in Hollywood under contract to producer Samuel Goldwyn, who felt some Parisian panache during the economic downturn would keep cinema relevant. He was not necessarily wrong, as the 1930s became a golden age for glamour in Hollywood, but Chanel's experience away from Paris was miserable. Chanel worked on just three films for Goldwyn: *Palmy Days* (1931), *Tonight or Never* (1931) and *The Greeks Had a Word for Them* (1932). She arrived late on the Eddie Cantor comedy *Palmy Days*, providing only a handful of gowns for Charlotte Greenwood and, infamously, four versions of the same dress for Barbara Weeks. Chanel wanted the dress to look its finest from every angle, when the actress was sitting, walking or standing; Weeks's scenes had to be shot in short takes while she changed into another variation of, to all intents and purposes, the same costume. With this one act, Chanel demonstrated that Hollywood was not for her. She was a fashion designer: clothes would never be costumes. Chanel's experience on *Tonight or Never* was no more harmonious, with the designer demanding star Gloria Swanson drop weight to fit in her clothes (Swanson was secretly pregnant at the time). *The Greeks Had a Word for Them* was

p50 left This impeccable hunting outfit created for *La Règle du Jeu* (*The Rules of the Game*) is characteristic of Chanel daywear: masculine in aesthetic, tailored and functional

—

p50 right Twenties-era Chanel clothes were created to be practical as well as fashionable

—

p51 Chanel's gowns for *Tonight or Never* were audacious in the extreme. This particular dress was featured in a *Photoplay* magazine article promoting Gloria Swanson's costumes

Chanel's final outing in Hollywood, and while it probably reflected her most concise work, she could not leave America quick enough.

Goldwyn hired Chanel to be more than a costume designer; he wanted someone to anticipate the fashions of Paris before they hit. Even the great Coco Chanel could not forecast an entire industry. However, in *Tonight or Never*, predicting what Paris – and thus eventually the world – would wear in six months' time was exactly what Chanel and Metro-Goldwyn-Mayer (MGM) attempted. Gloria Swanson plays opera singer Nella Vargo, a stroppy prima donna longing for love. Chanel's 'designed and executed' credit was one of the first to roll. Swanson was always known for being an ornately decorated clothes horse, but at this point her career was on the wane. Nonetheless she puts in a charming performance, and the Chanel costumes, while clearly struggling with Swanson's more rounded figure, look majestic. They feel modern. Not just the incredible fur and sequin ensembles, but also Chanel's undoubted forte – daywear. Nella's floral-print silk jersey jumpsuit with scoop neck, scalloped bell sleeves and big sparkly belt buckle has been referenced in practically every decade since. When travelling at night by train, Nella dons a lightweight double-breasted jacket and matching straight-line skirt, worn with club collar shirt spread over the jacket lapels and a bucket hat. The outfit, among all the evening showstoppers, exemplifies Chanel's real quest: comfort. Yet because Chanel did not know about Swanson's pregnancy during the shoot, she initially refused the actress's pleas to wear a specially made elasticized corset to hold her bump in. A corset-type garment of any description went against Chanel's ethos in fashion, but it was more important that her creations in *Tonight or Never* appear at their very best, for her, and for the studio funding her one million dollar contract.

Photoplay magazine ran an illustrated spread before the film was released showing off 'the latest Chanel' (costume apparently indistinguishable from fashion). The focus was Swanson's most extravagant gowns. One in particular, a long black velvet dress with wing drapery sleeves, jewelled clips to the shoulders and a split skirt is worn during a long scene in which Nella glides from room to room, quite appropriately, like a bat. With its extremely complex bodice and sleeve design, it seems more suitable for a dancehall or nightclub. Later Nella is wrapped in a satin and chinchilla fur coat with colossal upturned shawl collar and barrel cuffs over a silk and sequin-jewelled chemise, merely to keep warm while dining outside. In the final scene, Nella makes her big entrance in a black satin coat with double ermine collar, ermine barrel cuffs (again) and ermine muff. Chanel delivered exactly the breathtaking luxury that Goldwyn wanted.

DIANE VON FÜRSTENBERG

TAXI DRIVER (1976)
AMERICAN HUSTLE (2013)

Diane von Fürstenberg in New York, 1970. Fürstenberg is
as sensational as the clothes she creates, an aspirational
figurehead for the brand
—
p52 Cybill Shepherd looking every inch the independent
DVF woman in *Taxi Driver*

Diane von Fürstenberg's wrap dress is entirely dependent on the fluidity of the female body; it only exists off the hanger. In any context, the wrap dress personifies the contemporary woman. Nowhere is this more apparent than in *Taxi Driver* (1976) – the first time Von Fürstenberg's creation appears on screen. Cybill Shepherd's independent twenty-something Betsy is the DVF wearer incarnate.

In the film, loner Travis Bickle (Robert De Niro) drives a cab around New York at night, witnessing nothing but the worst of the city. Betsy is his ray of light in a life shrouded by darkness. Even director Martin Scorsese referred to her as the 'embodiment of goodness and beauty'. Costume designer Ruth Myers understood there was no more suitable garment for Betsy to wear than a wrap dress. Taken off the peg in 1975, Betsy's dress is an Art Nouveau swirled coral print on white silk jersey with a stand collar, long sleeves and button cuffs. Betsy wears a DVF wrap because it is comfortable and practical. She can eat in it, date in it and work in it. Travis worships her in this dress, though he doesn't ogle. To him, Betsy is all women, from friend to mother to lover.

Diane von Fürstenberg launched her wrap dress in 1974 after spotting two of her own line separates, a wrap top and plain skirt, worn on television by

p54 A contemporary update on the classic DVF wrap at a Diane von Fürstenberg show, Mercedes-Benz Fashion Week, Autumn 2015

—

p55 top Cybill Shepherd in a coral Diane von Fürstenberg wrap dress in *Taxi Driver*. The DVF wrap dress is designed to do anything in: work, play, even lunch with Robert De Niro

—

p55 bottom The chocolate feather-print wrap dress worn by Amy Adams in *American Hustle* was specially sourced by costume designer Michael Wilkinson

the daughter of Richard Nixon, then US president. She combined the top and skirt into a single garment, in the same manner as sportswear designer Claire McCardell had created her 'popover' dress 30 years before, though the popover was a wrapped housedress worn unaccompanied or as a top layer, while Von Fürstenberg's wrap is more a nightgown with one side swathed across the other and then tied or buttoned behind or at the hip.

In 1976, the same year *Taxi Driver* was released, Von Fürstenberg was featured on the front cover of *Newsweek* in her green and white twig-print wrap. This unexpectedly significant portrait of the era, precursor to the subsequent decade's women-in-business boom, stayed in the mind of director David O. Russell, who insisted costume designer Michael Wilkinson track down this dress for his 2013 film *American Hustle*. Set in 1978, *American Hustle* features Amy Adams as con artist Sydney Prosser, aka Lady Edith Greensly, who collates her wardrobe from abandoned garments in a dry cleaner's. Adams dons four DVF wraps in the movie, including the *Newsweek* green twig, which was found in an LA vintage store, plus what Wilkinson describes as white 'feather on chocolate', a contemporary black and red leopard print, and a briefly seen red utility. The turquoise wrap Adams wears is not DVF at all, but vintage Bob Mackie, while the slinky grey twist-front dress is contemporary Halston; Adams's snakeskin jersey garment is a vintage wrap top and pants – no label.

There are two fundamental types of DVF wrap: the 'Jeanne', with long cuffed sleeves and a stand collar, and the collarless 'Julian', sporting cuffless three-quarter or cap sleeves. All the DVF dresses in *American Hustle* are 'Jeanne's, as was Cybill Shepherd's in *Taxi Driver*. Arguably, the most coveted DVF, 'Jeanne' fuses a formalwear collar with a showstopper evening-wear décolletage.

In director Pedro Almodóvar's *The Skin I Live In* (*La piel que habito*, 2011), a geometric tube-print DVF is worn by Elena Anaya's transsexual character when she steps out for the first time after sex reassignment surgery. What better way to announce her arrival than in the pinnacle of sartorial femininity? (Amusingly, for a designer known for garments so defined by gender conventions, Von Fürstenberg trained in what was at the time the traditionally masculine field of electronics.) Almodóvar also used a DVF wrap for his 2009 film *Broken Embraces* (*Los abrazos rotos*). Penélope Cruz's character is based on an amalgamation of several 'jet set' fashion designers, Von Fürstenberg included. Lauren Graham wore two DVFs in glossy rom-com *Because I Said So* (2007). Television too is a natural home for DVF, worn mostly by professional-type characters as a signifier of success. There's nowhere Diane von Fürstenberg's timeless dress doesn't fit in.

DOLCE & GABBANA

ROMEO AND JULIET (1996)
UNDER SUSPICION (2000)
PHONE BOOTH (2002)
THE SKIN I LIVE IN (2011)

Stefano Gabbana and Domenico Dolce with Monica Bellucci in 2011. Bellucci first met the duo in 1990 and has been associated with the brand's marketing ever since
—
p56 Long-time muse of Dolce & Gabanna Monica Bellucci, wearing an elegant black satin D&G evening dress in *Under Suspicion*

D o not doubt Domenico Dolce and Stefano Gabbana's ability to surprise; they like to keep fashion on its toes. Their appearance on film charts their evolutionary nature, from flashy, even tacky origins, to the epitome of black-dress chic in the noughties, and beyond.

The brand's biggest splash on screen came courtesy of costume designer Kym Barrett for *Romeo and Juliet* (1996). Director Baz Luhrmann worked with Barrett to bring his updated version of Shakespeare's tale to life. He relocated the story to contemporary Los Angeles amidst a surge in street violence, and separated Romeo and Juliet's two warring families into rival gangs. Barrett used Dolce & Gabbana – principally their diffusion line, 'D&G', launched in 1994 – as inspiration and costume for the Capulet gang, headed by 'Prince' Tybalt (John Leguizamo). As a contrast, she dressed the Montague gang in loud Hawaiian punk. They are all teenagers pretending to be grown-ups, yet crying out to be kids, their attire both a uniform and a desperate need to be noticed.

Tybalt's main outfit is a black single-breasted suit with wide padded shoulders, over a zipped waistcoat bearing an image of Jesus Christ, with a black leather belt with silver circular buckle, and black Cuban boots with silver heels. The Capulet and Montague members are accessorized with pistol holsters, their guns decorated in Shakespearian and religious imagery. This iconography is carried throughout their overall look: Tybalt wears the Jesus vest, a gang member has a crucifix shaved in the back of his head, another has 'Sins' etched on his silver teeth. This is Wild West via a West Coast deluge of diffusion lines. Such lines were intended to broaden a designer brand's appeal, to make them more affordable and attainable for the youth market; regrettably, in most cases they lessened the appeal of the main brand, saturating high streets with enormous garish logos. Although the 'D&G' line folded in 2012, it received an early boost from *Romeo and Juliet*. The film was a huge success, initiating a cinematic resurgence in Shakespeare and legitimacy for exhibitionist fashion, particularly on men. Beginning with the simple black suit in *Reservoir Dogs* (1993), movies continued to refine this style as a nod to flamboyance.

Dolce & Gabbana met Monica Bellucci in 1990, kick-starting her international modelling career. It is debatable who has benefitted more from this relationship; she gave the glitzy label panache when it was striving to rebrand, and they gave her a career. *Under Suspicion* (2000) represents the perfect marriage of muse and artist, with Bellucci costumed as a positive stereotype of the voluptuous Italian ice queen Anita Ekberg in *La Dolce Vita* (1960). Dolce and Gabbana are both outspoken designers and, as such, controversial as a brand, yet they could never be accused of promoting unhealthy body types. Their very first collection in 1985 was entitled 'Real Women', and Bellucci is emblematic of just that.

As Chantal, the jealous wife of sleazy public official Henry Hearst (Gene Hackman), Bellucci is given one of the most voyeuristic reveals in the history of cinema: shot from behind, minus undergarments, halfway into a full-length black stretch-satin Dolce & Gabbana evening gown. As the story takes place over one night with flashbacks, Bellucci's primary costume is the black satin gown, a matching wrap added soon after her character's introduction, accessorized with large diamond drop earrings. Bellucci walks in the dress as if strutting down a catwalk, neatly befitting Chantal's keen awareness of her own sex appeal. The dress itself spearheaded Dolce & Gabbana's segue into spotless elegance. The fabric is heavy and shiny but unadorned, and the shoulder straps are fine and hinged like a bra, differing from the minimal spaghetti straps aimed at a younger market. Due to the dominance of Italian fashion during this period, Hollywood readily associated it with quality. For example, dialogue in the movie references Gene Hackman's character as wearing Armani. In fact, his clothes were provided by German brand Hugo Boss, but the intimation is clear – moneyed folk wear Italian. Towards the end of the film, Bellucci sports her final change, a black slash-neck top with plunging back and matching wiggle skirt. Again, the shape is designed

to enhance the actress's curves rather than hide them, unlike the previous decade's more slender silhouette.

Colin Farrell, as entertainment publicist Stu Shepard, wears a Dolce & Gabbana suit in *Phone Booth* (2002). Stu is selfish and conceited, destined to crash, which unfortunately personified the perception of the Dolce & Gabbana brand at this point. Yet perhaps this is too harsh an observation; fashionista film director Pedro Almodóvar did use a floral Dolce & Gabbana dress to imply overt femininity for the finale of *The Skin I Live In* (*La piel que habito*, 2011), whereby Vera (Elena Anaya) has forcibly changed sex from a man to a woman and is choosing to embrace the transformation (see also page 127). Dolce & Gabbana is whatever cinema needs it to be.

p58 Costumes for the 'Capulet' gang in *Romeo and
Juliet* took inspiration from the loud and flashy (and
now defunct) 'D&G' diffusion line
—
p59 top Colin Farrell in Dolce & Gabbana suit and gaudy
fuchsia shirt for *Phone Booth*
—
p59 right A ruched floral Dolce & Gabbana dress from
The Skin I Live In: supreme femininity for Vera's defining
act as a woman

DONNA KARAN

GREAT EXPECTATIONS (1998)
THE DEVIL WEARS PRADA (2006)

Donna Karan and Louis del'Olio at her 7th Avenue atelier in New York, 1979. Karan worked for Anne Klein before setting up her own house in 1985

—

p60 Everything Gwyneth Paltrow wears in *Great Expectations* is a shade of green – a colour the film's director Alfonso Cuarón admits to being obsessed with

Donna Karan represents a specific era defined by a specific outfit: the eighties power suit. Karan, born Donna Faske, did not invent the power suit, that sturdily structured garment designed to turn its wearer into a symbol, much like Bruce Wayne in his emblematic *Batman* costume, but she brought it to the masses.

To date, Donna Karan and her diffusion line 'DKNY' have appeared on screen only in shopped form, with all ensembles selected by costume designers and adapted later, or occasionally in-house. Most are random wardrobe pieces, such as selected female attire for the principals in *The Gingerbread Man* (1998). In 2009, 'DKNY' self-produced a short film starring Christina Ricci called *Four Play*. A sparse sixties-inspired promo for their 'Eldridge' handbag, the resulting two-minute mini-movie is light on narrative but heavy on style. Mostly, however, Donna Karan in cinema belongs to legacy. *Working Girl* (1985), the tale of a harassed Brooklyn secretary's transition to corporate Manhattanite, may not feature the brand in a literal sense, but without it costumier Ann Roth could not have created such a deliberately imposing silhouette, aped in real-life offices for the remainder of the decade.

Based on the Charles Dickens novel of 1861, director Alfonso Cuarón's contemporary update of *Great Expectations* (1998) garnered a considerable

p62 Donna Karan costume sketch for Gwyneth Paltrow in *Great Expectations*

—

p63 left Donna Karan fashion show during Mercedes-Benz Fashion Week, Autumn 2015. A minimal yet imposing and powerful silhouette still rules Karan's collections

—

p63 right Meryl Streep in *The Devil Wears Prada* wears a Donna Karan trench coat that intentionally matches her character's shock white hair

amount of press coverage for Donna Karan's involvement. Costume designer Judianna Makovsky clothed the entire cast, but Donna Karan provided several ensembles for Paltrow to wear in the part of Estella. Cuarón was adamant about using the colour green as an emotive theme throughout, for production design, costumes, even the opening titles. Within the context of the story, green is poisonous and decaying, like the crumbling Dinsmoor mansion owned by Estella's guardian. It also represents envy and growth, as experienced by central character Finn (Ethan Hawke) and Estella herself. Makovsky found it freeing to use so much of the colour; green is a subtle shade, similar to the warmth and cool of black and white. Cuarón had employed the colour to the same degree for his previous film, *A Little Princess* (1995), also with costume design by Makovsky.

Judianna Makovsky contacted Donna Karan's PR department directly because she had seen a garment the designer created for the catwalk and felt it would be perfect for *Great Expectations* – a green burnout velvet dress. With a modest costume budget, Makovsky could only borrow the dress and what came to be six others that Donna Karan provided, including a much-publicized asymmetric wiggle skirt and matching open shirt top. Karan even remade the evening gown Paltrow wears, as it would not fit off the rack. Though this was the extent of the brand's involvement in the film, the Donna Karan look absolutely personifies the regal, debutante character of Paltrow's Estella.

As Miranda Priestley, editor-in-chief of *Runaway* magazine (said to be based on Anna Wintour of US *Vogue*) in *The Devil Wears Prada* (2006), Meryl Streep is dressed head to toe in practically anything but Prada. Streep's white trench coat was sourced by costumier Patricia Field and supplied by Donna Karan, whose association with women who have broken through the glass ceiling is an obvious allusion to Priestley's own success.

For *Bernard and Doris* (2006), loosely based on the true story of tobacco billionairess Doris Duke (played by Susan Sarandon), Donna Karan allowed the raiding of the brand's extensive archives to costume and accessorize Sarandon. The film was made for a mere $750,000. Without Karan's assistance, Doris's requisite opulent look would not have been so convincing. In *National Treasure 2: Book of Secrets* (2007), Judianna Makovsky returned to Donna Karan to procure a black leather biker jacket – one of her favourite costume choices in the movie – for fashion-conscious actress Diane Kruger as Dr Abigail Chase. Again, a successful woman represented by an equivalent brand.

Power dressing was not invented in the eighties; women of the forties had already begun this movement before anyone had a name for it. Yet thanks to designers like Donna Karan, Giorgio Armani and Ralph Lauren, it became aspirational and accessible to all women where it was needed most – in the business world. No Donna Karan, no Working Girl.

ELSA SCHIAPARELLI

EVERY DAY'S A HOLIDAY (1937)
MOULIN ROUGE (1952)
W.E. (2011)

Elsa Schiaparelli in 1951. Not as conventionally attractive or glamorous as her closest rival Coco Chanel, Schiaparelli was an artist and dressmaking her canvas
—
p64 Zsa Zsa Gabor in *Moulin Rouge* wearing one of the most Schiaparelli dresses in the film, though the design itself is actually based on a Paquin creation

Elsa Schiaparelli was an avant-garde designer responsible for some of the most spectacular and diverse dresses and hats of all time – creations that are still very much a fashion influence today – though hers is far from a household name. (Of course, this may have a little something to do with that fact that most people cannot pronounce it: 'scap-a-reli', by the by.)

Diminutive in stature, Schiaparelli made clothes to be seen, in bright colours with high waists, visible zippers and broad shoulders. She was strongly influenced by abstract art, particularly surrealism, mainly via her friend Salvador Dalí. Like Dalí, Schiaparelli enjoyed playing with interpretation and perception. She used fabric trickery to make this concept come alive in several of her garments. One of Schiaparelli's most famous creations, the 'Tears' dress, an ensemble of evening gown and head-veil from her 1938 'Circus' collection, sported 'rips' in the veil that were actually intentional openings in the fabric lined with silk, while the print on the evening gown – designed especially for Schiaparelli by Dalí – used trompe l'oeil for a similar effect. Although Schiaparelli was known for her dramatic hat and dress creations (unlike her rival Coco Chanel, Schiaparelli had a sense of humour about fashion), widespread recognition came from the relatively down-to-earth hand-knitted

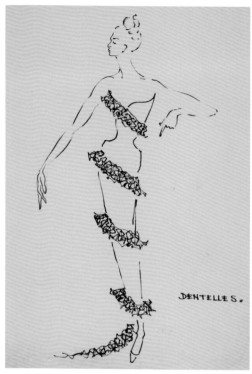

Sketch of a Schiaparelli evening dress showing similar
features to her reworked Paquin gown for *Moulin Rouge*

Schiaparelli was known for her outlandish hats; she even
created one in the shape of an upside-down shoe

'Cravat' sweater, which gained popularity in the early
thirties. Schiaparelli's true mainstay, however, would
always be the daring and the bizarre.

Oddly, several British films featured
Schiaparelli's name in the thirties. Odd because
Italian-born Schiaparelli was living in Paris at the
time, but also because the movie industry would not
be considered artistically fulfilling for a renowned
couturière, even one like Schiaparelli who was, in
point of fact, untrained. Some of the British productions she contributed garments to, such as *The Tunnel*
(1935) and *Brewster's Millions* (1935) – for which she
was actually uncredited – are better known than
others. One particularly intriguing project was
The Beloved Vagabond (1936), a slight musical drama
made at Ealing Studios that remains barely seen or
discussed today.

Schiaparelli collaborated with costumier
Ernst Stern in providing gowns for *The Beloved
Vagabond*, which was shot simultaneously in English
and French. The story is primarily set in 1900, the tale
of Gaston (Maurice Chevalier), a Frenchman who
moves from London to his native France and, as a
peculiar act of honour, lives as a tramp. Schiaparelli's
costumes are almost entirely reserved for Gaston's

wealthy lost love Joanna, played by Betty Stockfeld,
including what appears to be a pink or red leather coat,
striking enough to make characters around her double take, with colossal pagoda sleeves (a favourite of
Schiaparelli) shaped behind her neck and shoulders
like a giant sea shell. Joanna's final outfit, worn for
a dinner party, is made from metallic lamé, sporting
bulbous puff sleeves indicative of the period. Another
gown that may or may not be Schiaparelli's is seen
on Margaret Lockwood as Blanquette, a fellow tramp
Gaston meets roaming the French countryside. Most
telling is the wide sash worn around her waist and tied
at the rear, closely resembling a specific detail on a
summer dress from Schiaparelli's 'Parachute' collection created the same year. Costumes in *The Beloved
Vagabond* are glamorous and eye-catching and, as
such, generally out of context with the movie itself.
Schiaparelli seemingly used cinema to experiment
more than anything else.

Hollywood was not exactly Schiaparelli's
true calling. She was popular with all major female
stars of the thirties, such as Ginger Rogers, Katharine
Hepburn and Vivien Leigh. However, Schiaparelli's
work on screen was a diminished version of her house
style; sometimes it was hardly even her own. Mae

Schiaparelli was at a creative peak when Mae West
contracted her for *Every Day's a Holiday*

The gowns Schiaparelli provided for *Every Day's a Holiday*
required considerable altering as no fittings ever took place

West was a client of Schiaparelli, and insisted that she
provide gowns for her comedy *Every Day's a Holiday*
(1937). At the time West could not travel to Paris for
fittings, and Schiaparelli refused to travel to Hollywood.
As a compromise, West sent her measurements to
Schiaparelli from which she built a dress form to
design on. This form was purportedly the inspiration
for Schiaparelli's first perfume, 'Shocking' – possibly
a reference to West's larger than expected dimensions.
Creatively, Schiaparelli was in a fine place; around
this time, she created her bug necklace (part of her
1938 'Pagan' collection) and celebrated shoe hat with
Dalí. However, something got lost in transit with *Every
Day's a Holiday*. Whether due to West's increasing
weight (though she is notably trimmer in the final
film) or Schiaparelli's imprecision, practically nothing fit, and the ensembles Schiaparelli sent had to
be almost completely reworked. Some of West's
outfits even sported the label 'United Costumers Inc.
Manufacturers', with no mention of Schiaparelli at
all. This was typical for costumes during the thirties,
and many were tagged with just a handwritten label;
Schiaparelli, however, would be unlikely to send her
clothes – especially those she exclusively designed –
anywhere unlabelled and unsigned.

Though she may not have been a perfect match
for *Every Day's a Holiday*, Schiaparelli was a natural
fit for *Moulin Rouge* (1952), based on artist Henri de
Toulouse-Lautrec's bygone world of tortured artistic
integrity and voyeuristic debauchery. Marcel Vertès
was overall costumier, with Schiaparelli designing
for Zsa Zsa Gabor as real-life can-can dancer Jane
Avril. Schiaparelli's dresses for Gabor were all based
on actual posters featuring Avril that Lautrec had
sketched for the Moulin Rouge cabaret club in Paris.
Although Gabor was far more voluptuous than her
character's real-life counterpart, her costumes – six
changes in total – evoked the spirit of Lautrec's drawings while stopping short of being direct copies.

Schiaparelli had worked with Vertès before;
as an illustrator, he helped design her perfume bottles.
Vertès also duplicated all the Lautrec posters and
artwork featured in *Moulin Rouge*. Apart from an early
fitted red dress with mammoth shocking-pink bow that
just screamed Schiaparelli, Gabor's most famous
costume features far later in the story. Avril accompa-
nies Lautrec to (Jeanne) Paquin's boutique, hoping to
purchase something special for an upcoming performance. By this point, Avril has become a big star and
needs a showstopper. The dress she chooses is

Zsa Zsa Gabor barely resembled Jane Avril, but her *Moulin Rouge* costumes accurately recreate the dancer's outfits

Costume designer Arianne Phillips made several gowns for Andrea Riseborough's Wallis Simpson in *W.E.* based on actual Schiaparelli gowns from the era

practically identical to an 1899 Lautrec poster for the Moulin Rouge: a black and red full-length sheath with tulle hem and sequin snake coiled from thighs to midriff, its head resting on the bust. In essence, this is a Paquin gown sketched by Lautrec and copied by Schiaparelli – an extraordinarily modern ensemble in 1900. It is so Schiaparelli though, the winding snake especially, a kooky, Asian-influenced touch that fit perfectly into her world. This was very much something she might have designed for her own collection in the mid- to late thirties (somewhat evoking her 1938 'Skeleton' dress). *Moulin Rouge* won an Academy Award for Marcel Vertès, with hardly any recognition for Schiaparelli: a pity because, unlike some – perhaps most – collaborations between fashion and costume designers, this was genuine teamwork that tapped into both artists' talents.

Elsa Schiaparelli continues to exert an influence in cinema. Arianne Phillips recreated more than one Schiaparelli gown for Andrea Riseborough as Wallis Simpson in *W.E.* (2011). Simpson was a client of Schiaparelli, wearing her legendary lobster dress in a photograph taken by Cecil Beaton in 1937 and published in *Vogue*. The print designed was by Dalí; apparently he was keen to cover the entire fabric in mayonnaise, but on consideration even Schiaparelli thought that might be too much. Her work has become a byword for zaniness in fashion. Costumier Judianna Makovsky referenced Schiaparelli for the Capitol costumes in science-fiction drama *The Hunger Games* (2012), appreciating how the designer's extravagant flair would suit the futuristic city.

Zsa Zsa Gabor in a Schiaparelli design, based on a Toulouse-
Lautrec poster, to play Jane Avril in *Moulin Rouge*

FENDI

CONVERSATION PIECE (1974)
THE AGE OF INNOCENCE (1993)
BEDAZZLED (2000)
THE ROYAL TENENBAUMS (2001)

Karl Lagerfeld at a drawing board in Germany in 1984.
Lagerfeld essentially made the Fendi brand by launching
its first ready-to-wear label

—

p70 Michelle Pfeiffer In *The Age of Innocence*. Fur has
long been used in cinema as a means of portraying wealth
and status

Fendi is intrinsically linked to cinema. The house is keen to emphasize the collaborative nature of their contributions to film, which at present number over 30 features. They are not costume designers; they work with costume designers. They understand what a Fendi garment means on screen, and are happy to embrace all connotations, from a delectable mink coat worn by Madonna in *Evita* (1996) to a garish red fur jacket with patent leather trim, and red leather boots, on Elizabeth Hurley in *Bedazzled* (2000). Even outside of cinema, Fendi's clothes are as much about costume as fashion. They delineate a certain type of person: sometimes exquisite, sometimes kitsch, but always rich.

Fendi began life in 1918 when Adele Casagrande set up a leather and fur workshop in Rome. In 1925 Adele married Edoardo Fendi and they opened a boutique next door selling their own goods during the post-war recovery period. In 1946 Adele and Edoardo's five daughters joined the family business. Yet most significant to the Fendi story was the appointment of Karl Lagerfeld as creative director in 1965. Lagerfeld moulded Fendi into what it is today: a luxury fashion conglomerate. His belief in 'fur as material' – using the fabric beyond mere accessory to construct entire garments, namely divine fur coats – made Fendi famous. In 1977 Lagerfeld launched Fendi's first ready-to-wear

collection. Today he is supported by Adele's grand-daughter, Silvia Venturini Fendi, who joined the company in 1987, becoming creative director of accessories in 1994. She was responsible for the hugely successful launch of the 'Baguette' bag in 1997, a commercial triumph that marked Fendi as a key player in the luxury goods market.

Nonetheless, were it not for one particular film – *Conversation Piece* (*Gruppo di famiglia in un interno*), released in 1974 – Fendi may not have moved beyond furs and leatherwear. Before *Conversation Piece* the house had produced only accessories and one-off frocks. Fendi made bespoke furs for the film under the guidance of costumier Piero Tosi, and on the insistence of star Silvana Mangano, they designed the rest of her wardrobe, too. This encouraged Fendi to produce an official ready-to-wear collection in 1977 – their '365' line, 'a dress for every day of the year' – which was a huge success.

With such a deep-rooted history in cinema, it is hardly surprising that in 2013 Fendi held an exhibition to celebrate their work in this field – 'Making Dreams: Fendi and the Cinema', staged at Rome's Cinema Manzoni. On show was everything from Silvana Mangano's astrakhan fur jacket to Gwyneth Paltrow's wrap-over mink from her role as Margot in *The Royal Tenenbaums* (2001). It was an unabashed love letter to the movies – and even more blatantly, to fur.

Despite the demonization of fur during the early eighties, it has a long-standing relationship with cinema that cannot be undone by a change in cultural attitudes. Fur represents the finest of everything, the pinnacle of upper class. Michelle Pfeiffer's Countess Olenska in *The Age of Innocence* (1993) and Marisa Berenson's matriarch Allegra Recchi in *I Am Love* (*Io sono l'amore*, 2009) are both women who are governed by the sartorial constructs of their social status. They wear Fendi fur to tell us what they are (wealthy), and who they are (elite, aloof, repressed). Nobility without fur is like a rapper without expensive trainers; it is non-conformity a step too far. Mangano's audacious Bianca Brumonti in *Conversation Piece* is draped in fur for practically every scene.

Symbolically, fur is a barrier to female genitalia; it covers or hides that which is most desired. Women who wear fur do so not only to suggest wealth but also sexual exclusivity. In *The Royal Tenenbaums*, troubled genius Margot's fur coat is both a rejection and acknowledgement of her status (see also page 102). Teaming a $4,000 coat with a Lacoste tennis dress denotes a more youthful and adventurous breed of Fendi wearer. Fendi will always symbolize money, but as costumier Karen Patch's use of that toffee-coloured mink on Margot demonstrates, it can do far more than just celebrate the bourgeoisie.

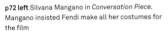

p72 left Silvana Mangano in *Conversation Piece*.
Mangano insisted Fendi make all her costumes for
the film
—

p72 right The famous toffee mink Fendi coat worn by
Gwyneth Paltrow in *The Royal Tenenbaums*. Yes, it was
real mink and worth around $4,000
—

p73 left Elizabeth Hurley wearing a red Fendi fur coat
designed by Deena Appel for *Bedazzled*
—

p73 right Fur continues to be a feature of Fendi's
collections, including this typically extravagant coat
from Winter 2015

Protean in its connotations, the Fendi name
can be all things to all people. While Allegra Recchi
represents an ageing grand dame to whom Fendi is a
watchword for elegance and distinction, the male characters in *I Am Love* wear the brand as a badge of nondescript unity. This is very much the Fendi Milanese way;
belonging is far more important than individuality.

GILBERT ADRIAN

GRAND HOTEL (1932)
LETTY LYNTON (1932)
THE WOMEN (1939)
THE WIZARD OF OZ (1939)

Gilbert Adrian, known professionally as Adrian, about 1930, when he was still under contract at MGM

—

p74 Judy Garland as Dorothy in *The Wizard of Oz* wearing one of the most famous movie costumes in history

Born in 1903, Adrian came from a family of milliners but honed his own craft as a costume designer on Broadway. From there he went to work for director Cecil B. DeMille, who in essence invented the concept of costume design – the notion that garments should be specifically created to function in context on film. However, it was after moving with DeMille to Metro-Goldwyn-Mayer (MGM) that Adrian's true calling as cinema's luxury couturier really became apparent. After creating costumes at the studio for 13 years during Hollywood's golden age of beauty and exuberance, Adrian left to open his own fashion house.

MGM's *Letty Lynton* (1932) is generally thought to be among Adrian's most important onscreen work, yet due to a copyright dispute the film has hardly been seen since its original release. The narrative revolves around New York socialite Letty Lynton, who gets away with murdering her lover. Adrian designed costumes for star Joan Crawford as Letty, with one ensemble in particular becoming known as the 'Letty Lynton dress': a dramatic, flouncy gown in white cotton organdie, featuring padded shoulders and ruffled puff sleeves. The dress was heavily copied, mainly by Macy's department store in New York, and many believe it defined the look of the era. Considering the dress was created by Adrian before a similar silhouette came to dominate the decade, this could be true, but is impossible to prove. *Flying Down to Rio* (1933), with costumes designed by Walter Plunkett and Irene, features a very similar puff-sleeve gown worn by Dolores del Río, and the film was a bigger box office hit than *Letty Lynton*. The thirties, particularly the later part of the decade, definitely featured a *Letty Lynton* look, but whether the movie itself created this trend or Adrian interpreted it from Paris is ultimately unclear.

The biggest movie of 1932 was unquestionably *Grand Hotel*. Starring Greta Garbo and Joan Crawford, with gowns by Adrian and a hefty budget upward of $700,000, *Grand Hotel* delivered total glamour when Hollywood needed it most. There was an all-star cast, but for costume buffs focus immediately fell on Garbo and Crawford, in two very different roles: Garbo is Grusinskaya, a Russian ballerina living a life of pampered luxury, while Crawford is Flaemmchen, a struggling stenographer willing to do anything to make her way, including sleeping with whomever she needs for the promise of a better life. Crawford only has three costumes for the entire film: a black dress with asymmetric lace ruffle collar and cuffs, double-breasted fastening (like a suit) and low-cut neckline; a lighter-colour day dress, calf-length with pleated hem and lightly padded shoulders; and a lace-trim peignoir

with matching negligée. Flaemmchen indicates in the narrative that the black dress was purchased for her, presumably by a lover. It forms a deliberately provocative silhouette, though is just demure enough to maintain Crawford's character as someone who needs and likes sex but is not standing on street corners. With Grusinskaya's more sumptuous wardrobe featuring gargantuan fur coats and a stunning flared-sleeve chiffon gown just to swan about her hotel room in, we are supposed to feel worse for Flaemmchen. Yet she is in far more control of her life than dreamily pathetic Grusinskaya. Adrian's costumes are not a showcase but make sense contextually, particularly because they are not too over the top. They are fashionably on point without overly dating features, although Garbo's lamé robe with mandarin collar, padded shoulders and batwing sleeves only seems in place to give the actress a memorable entrance – at least more memorable than Crawford's. When Flaemmchen strolls into the lobby in her black dress and white gloves, no one bats an eyelid. Adrian was not solely focused on dramatic details; he designed for his stars and for their characters, but most crucially for the narrative.

Due to clothing designs being so blatantly copied by department stores, costumiers such as Adrian, Walter Plunkett and Bernard Newman came

Adrian created all three of Joan Crawford's costumes for *Grand Hotel*, including this black dress that contrasts with the over-the-top luxury of Greta Garbo's character

Adrian's gowns for *The Women*. The 10-minute Technicolor fashion sequence featuring some of his most astonishing designs was cut from the film but has since been restored

Adrian's dress for Joan Crawford in *Letty Lynton*. The dress
was said to influence Paris fashion throughout the thirties

to have their work publicized through Cinema Fashion Shops. These shops were put in place by the Modern Merchandising Bureau with the specific intention of selling approved lines dictated by major studios. Sketches and photographs were taken of stars in costume, sometimes up to a year before a film was released, and clothing and accessories were then made up and sold in stores as a form of advance promotion. Case in point for these new fashion-endorsed movies was *The Women* (1939), which despite being shot in black and white featured a ten-minute Technicolor sequence that was basically a catwalk of Adrian's latest creations, apparently forced on director George Cukor by the studio. It is not difficult to see why Cukor might object. The show serves no narrative purpose whatsoever; it is only in place to sell Adrian.

The Wizard of Oz (1939) was a seminal film for MGM, with its explosive use of Technicolor and a career-making turn for their teen starlet Judy Garland as Dorothy. Adrian's contribution is often reduced to Dorothy's blue gingham pinafore dress worn over a short puff-sleeve blouse and a pair of ruby-red sequined slippers. In actual fact, the designer made over 3,000 costume sketches requiring a mammoth team of seamstresses, fitters and shoemakers. Five pairs of the slippers are known to have survived today, though more pop up at auction from time to time. Different versions were made – at least seven – for

various shots: one pair with gleaming red soles that poked out from underneath the fallen house, another covered in orange felt to dampen sound as Dorothy skipped along the yellow brick road. Likewise, several incarnations of the gingham dress were created, even one in grey for the film's sepia sequence, and another entirely different version with curled-toe shoes for Garland's make-up and costume tests. Garland was seventeen at the time of shooting, playing a 12-year-old. Her breasts were bound to flatten them, and kept in place by a panel sewn into the rear of the dress. It was a hellish production for Adrian and his team to prep, and a nightmare for Garland to shoot. Examined in close-up, the dress itself is poorly made with uneven seams and stitching. One could argue that this is intentional, that in context the dress of a farm girl would be poorly made. It is more likely, however, that such details could and did miss his meticulous eye, especially in this simple costume, so unlike the grand silk sheaths Adrian designed for his favourites Katharine Hepburn and Joan Crawford.

In 1941, Adrian left MGM and set up Adrian Ltd. in Beverly Hills. This was a time when, due to wartime disruption of trade in Europe, America had a real chance to lead fashion with their more easy-going, casual style. Nonetheless, it was initially a tough slog for Adrian, with his name carrying only so much weight away from the studio. Eventually he had

p78 Judy Garland's costume as Dorothy in *The Wizard of Oz* was a basic gingham cotton pinafore. At least seven different versions of the dress were made for various shots in the film

—

p79 Though most of the attention to Adrian's work on *The Wizard of Oz* is focused on Garland's Dorothy costume, he also created all the Munchkins' outfits, primarily constructed of soft felt

a breakthrough with a relatively simple drop-waist black dress, a vast bow wrapped around the thigh area of the skirt marking it as evening attire. Adrian became known for his black dresses, often in hourglass forms, constructed of modern Rayon crepe or even cotton. As with his time at MGM, he still found many of his designs copied for the mass-produced market, perhaps because he developed collections around easily identifiable 'themes', in essence similar to costume design. Despite Adrian's consummate skill, he was better at reading and refining trends than setting them. Although, bringing *Letty Lynton* into the equation, Adrian is perhaps far more important a tastemaker than he has ever given credit for.

GIORGIO ARMANI

AMERICAN GIGOLO (1980)
HANNA (2011)
THE WOLF OF WALL STREET (2013)
A MOST VIOLENT YEAR (2014)

Giorgio Armani in 1979 surrounded by drawings of his deconstructed suit that would dominate both male and female fashion in the early eighties
—
p80 Richard Gere in Armani for *American Gigolo*. The aesthetic is a mix of fitted early eighties form (trousers) and broad, almost triangular pre–World War II silhouette (jacket)

Credited with having contributed to 200-plus feature films, Giorgio Armani is a world-renowned fashion designer who launched his career creating the costume for Richard Gere in *American Gigolo* in 1980. Armani was sharp with this relationship, spinning it into a virtual catwalk that he has continued to utilize for nearly four decades now. A devotee of the grandiose cinema of Milan, where he grew up, Armani understands that the power of movies is perception. Fashion has never been about what is real; it is about desire.

Giorgio Armani dresses the empty individual on screen; he creates persona through clothes. Julian (Gere) in *American Gigolo* is only what he wears. A narcissistic lover for hire, Julian perceives all those without his expensive attire as beneath him. Director Paul Schrader brought Armani onboard because he wanted an up-and-coming fashion designer to reflect Julian's aspirational lifestyle. At the time, John Travolta was in place to star, but in retrospect it is difficult to imagine he could have done more to launch the Armani brand than Gere. Schrader pushed for a dandy Edwardian vibe, the strutting peacock. This is translated on screen as a forties silhouette of pleated trousers and long, broadly cut jackets, though with shoulder padding largely removed for a more deconstructed feel. Julian is supposed to be the epitome of effortless cool,

yet he is very aware of his own persona. Moreover, the one item of clothing he wears traditionally associated with this ideal, a plain black suit, is mocked in the film as 'funeral attire'. Odd then that towards the end of the eighties, Armani became renowned for his version of a plain black suit, white shirt and black tie – 'the Armani tux' – which is still celebrated today.

Having worked with fellow Italian designer Nino Cerruti, the young Giorgio Armani intended to concentrate on creating clothes that amplified a gentleman's muscular build – the classic 'V' shape. However, witnessing a move away from formal dressing in the seventies, he chose to imitate French ready-to-wear designer Daniel Hechter's relaxed and layered tailoring for both men and women instead.

Women wearing Armani is a byword in cinema for professional and independent. For his collaboration with costumier Lucie Bates on *Hanna* (2011), Armani was asked to provide key items for Cate Blanchett's character, Marissa. A CIA agent tasked with tracking down Hanna, the deadly daughter of a former operative, Marissa is cold and mercilessly driven. With the costume design of *Hanna* inspired by Grimm's fairy tales, Blanchett is symbolically the wicked witch, attired in greens and reds combined with serious office greys.

Bates selected items from Armani's then current 2010 collection but had to rework several pieces to closer fit the neurotic nature of Marissa's personality, particularly the colour of her signature coat. Marissa's often-seen high heels were purchased from an Armani store in Milan. She is an obsessive, as women who wear Armani on film tend to be – see also Jodie Foster as steely Armani-clad politician Delacourt in *Elysium* (2013). Right or wrong, women who achieve are dressed in Armani because of an inbuilt association with mannish tailoring. To succeed in a man's world, women must apparently adopt their silhouette.

Most of Giorgio Armani's collaborations come via star involvement – an actor will request the use of Armani because of their loyalty to the brand. Sometimes this can be harmonious, benefitting both Armani and the film itself, such as *Duplicity*, starring Armani's personal friend Clive Owen. At other times, a situation like that surrounding prohibition-era gangster thriller *The Untouchables* (1987) arises, whereby costume designer Marilyn Vance-Straker redesigned everything Armani provided because it was historically inaccurate and did not fit. For *The Wolf of Wall Street* (2013), costumier Sandy Powell worked with Armani on the insistence of lead actor Leonardo DiCaprio and

p82 left Cate Blanchett wearing an Armani coat in *Hanna*. The coat was originally designed by Armani in blue but was refashioned in green by costume designer Lucie Bates to better fit Blanchett's character

—

p82 right Two of Armani's suits feature in *The Wolf of Wall Street* along with selected separates, such as these pleated slacks worn by Leonardo DiCaprio with a Ralph Lauren polo shirt – 'new money' attire

—

p83 Set in 1981, *A Most Violent Year* stars Jessica Chastain as the enterprising wife of an up and coming New York businessman; she was dressed exclusively in Armani

director Martin Scorsese. Although Powell used only two Armani suits, this partnership did fulfil a narrative purpose. Armani's name is synonymous with ambition, so when Jordan Belfort (DiCaprio) is a young Wall Street trader he of course wears an Armani suit. Yet all the truly wealthy traders would choose bespoke. Later, now past their level, Jordan still wears Armani because he is 'new money'. This is what Powell helps to convey: Belfort rises from nothing to nouveau riche to rich; when he wears Armani it illustrates these junctures in the story.

Armani is one of the clearest examples of literal brand creation on film. With recent Hollywood projects such as the 1981-set crime drama *A Most Violent Year* (2014) and *The Dinner* (2017, again with Richard Gere), the designer continues to understand the benefit of costume collaborations in promoting his brand.

GUCCI

AMERICAN HUSTLE (2013)
RUSH (2013)

Aldo Gucci in 1977, eldest son of founder Guccio, largely credited with bringing the brand to mainstream success in the 1950s
—
p84 Apart from her wedding dress (sourced vintage), all of Olivia Wilde's costumes in *Rush* were supplied by Gucci

S ince its creation in 1921 by former hotel porter Guccio Gucci, the house of Gucci has skirted tremendous success and near failure. From its flourishing as the choice of leatherwear for the jet set during the fifties, to its peak as the utmost flashy designer label in the seventies, then artistic saturation throughout the eighties, revitalization at the hands of a young Tom Ford in the nineties, and to the present day – this has always been a brand in love with its heyday yet trying to forge an innovative future. The Gucci story is as dramatic as any of the films for which it has produced costumes, as evidenced by socialite Patrizia Reggiani hiring a hit man to murder her husband and heir to the Gucci empire, Maurizio. It is no wonder that at one point Martin Scorsese was considering making a movie of the whole sorry affair, as was Ridley Scott, with Angelina Jolie set to star as Patrizia.

Even more than Chanel, Gucci had realized the strength in brand identity. It is not enough just to wear Gucci; you have to tell everyone you are. The interlocking double-G emblem has been in use since the early sixties. Combine this emblem with the Gucci colour band of green-red-green stripe, and a status symbol is created. Not merely a name, but an actual physical manifestation of the name. The Gucci logo removes all doubt.

Olivia Wilde's shearling (fleece from a shearling sheep) coat in *Rush*. The same style was worn by her real-life character, model Suzy Miller

Gucci has appeared in several movies to date. Most are post-2000, following the brand's Tom Ford upsurge. In 2015, they provided and co-designed much of Blake Lively's enviable wardrobe with costumier Angus Strathie for *The Age of Adaline* – notably, Lively was the face of the brand at the time.

Although only glimpsed in *Silence of the Lambs* sequel *Hannibal* (2001), Gucci was cleverly employed by costume designer Janty Yates to reinforce Lecter's (Anthony Hopkins) actions within the story. Imprisoned Lecter derides trainee FBI agent Clarice during *Silence of the Lambs* for her 'good bag and cheap shoes'. Now escaped and on the run from Clarice in *Hannibal*, he leaves a box of Gucci stilettos inside her house; the subtext being she is now woman enough to wear the best, and for Lecter, lover of all things culturally European, that has to be Gucci.

Cosmopolis (2012) is Gucci on the screen by default. Costume designer Denise Cronenberg originally wanted leading man Robert Pattinson in Prada suits, but the label was not willing to supply her with any. Instead she approached Gucci, worn by Pattinson in real life, and they provided six identical black two-button single-breasted suits, white shirts, belts,

ties and shoes. Everything Pattinson's character – robotically anal broker Eric Packer – wears is by Gucci. It could be argued that this is not the best advertisement for a label that has always prided itself on creativeness, but there is no doubting Pattinson himself makes the suit far more desirable than the man he portrays. This is where a compromise has to be reached between a fashion house such as Gucci, looking to promote their product in a movie, and the requirements of the narrative. Why is the character wearing this brand, and what does it say about them? Most important of all, and certainly in the case of *Cosmopolis*, does this even matter? If Pattinson is beautiful in slim-fitting 'Signoria'-line Gucci, we are able to project ourselves onto his body. The consequence of which is we hopefully purchase the suit. That his character is a billionaire drone is immaterial; the important thing is he looks incredible.

There is a more evocative use of Gucci in 1970s-set true-life racing drama *Rush* (2013), although disappointingly little of the brand is actually seen, considering the amount of effort costumier Julian Day went to for their involvement. He scoured vintage Gucci archives, requesting then creative director Frida

Amy Adams in *American Hustle* wears a Gucci signature
horsebit necklace, based on an equestrian bridle snaffle,
as a sign of wealth

Giannini remake specific items for the film. Day's
concept was to use Gucci and fellow Italian house
Salvatore Ferragamo to imply the contrasting lifestyles
and personalities of *Rush*'s two leading men and their
partners, James Hunt (Chris Hemsworth) and Suzy
Miller (Olivia Wilde), and Niki Lauda (Daniel Brühl)
and Marlene Knaus (Alexandra Maria Lara). Hunt and
Miller were partygoers in glitzy Gucci, while subdued
Lauda and wife Marlene wore comparatively refined
Ferragamo. This is not easy to determine because
director Ron Howard was keener to showcase the
story's racing sequences than the drivers' lives away
from the track. Nonetheless, Gucci make an impression thanks to Olivia Wilde. Her character is a model,
so unsurprisingly treats the world as her catwalk. Case
in point, she arrives at a filthy garage workshop in a full-
length suede and fur-trimmed coat with a purple fedora,
feather tucked in the brim. It is aggressive pimp chic,
a real in-your-face entrance befitting of Gucci, who
were reputedly more than happy to be epitomized by
the actress. Wilde wears Gucci for all her scenes in
Rush, including sporting a black handbag with oversized double-G buckle. All except her wedding dress,
which Day sourced separately.

The gaudy overkill of seventies Gucci also
makes an appearance in *American Hustle* (2013),
chosen by costume designer Michael Wilkinson for
con artist Sydney Prosser (Amy Adams) in her guise
as 'Lady Edith Greensly', an English socialite who spe-
cializes in separating men from their wealth (see also
page 88). Edith's 'Lady Lock' handbag is a touch of brass
to sway her victims; likewise her horsebit necklace,
a signature piece introduced by Gucci in the 1950s to
recall their equestrian leather past. If Edith has money,
she can make her 'clients' money. Sydney creates Lady
Edith as a facade but struggles to reconcile money with
class. Old money never shouts, while Gucci is the sartorial definition of shouting as loudly as possible.

HALSTON

THE THOMAS CROWN AFFAIR (1999)
AMERICAN HUSTLE (2013)

Halston in his New York City office, 1970s
—
p88 Amy Adams in *American Hustle* wearing Halston
leather – costume designer Michael Wilkinson's personal
favourite ensemble from the film

Never has a label been so celebrated, maligned
and celebrated again as Halston. Roy Halston,
though he preferred just 'Halston', was by most
accounts a snobby prima donna in love with his own
reflection. He was also an era-encapsulating milliner
and dress designer. That era was the seventies, essentially the twenties redux; partying was rife, drugs
and alcohol were rifer. Everyone knew it could not
last. Halston clothed a figurative Last Days of Rome.
On screen his name represents someone utterly alive,
yet ripe for a fall.

A Halston-style frock is based on the designer's love of vintage fashion and cinema – generally a
Grecian gown, full of drape, made to skim a no-body
body rather than hug a curvy one. Echoing the thirties,
Halston employed backless cuts (after the previous
decade's fascination with exposing the legs) and halter
necklines in fabrics such as crepe de chine, jersey
silk and the hugely versatile Ultrasuede. He provided
some of these exact-style dresses for *The Wiz*'s (1978)
Emerald City sequence, which intentionally resembled
New York super-club – *the* nightclub of the seventies –
Studio 54. Halston and Studio 54 go hand in hand
because he dressed practically any woman famous
enough to be snapped gliding in there. His gowns were
created for posing and propping up the bar with a

cocktail, not fine dining and walks in the park. Using only the clingiest fabrics, they were unforgiving to all but the most willowy of figures. Happily for him, such figures went hand in hand with excessive drug use and hedonism. Even though Halston did not provide costumes for the crime thriller *Scarface* (1983), set in the early eighties, his influence is obvious in the costumes for lead actress Michelle Pfeiffer. Ironically, while the movie was in production, Halston's own business was nose-diving into decline.

Pfeiffer's character, sullen disco queen Elvira, is the ideal coat hanger for the Halston look. Her slim frame is swathed in shimmery chemises, typically backless, with spaghetti straps and a long slit up the leg. We see everything and nothing with a Halston dress; he directs the eye to expose the hidden sensuality of a naturally boyish figure. These are catwalk model clothes, intended for audacious display only. And nowhere was the display more audacious than on Rene Russo in *The Thomas Crown Affair* (1999). Her character dances sans underwear in a see-through Halston chemise at a black and white ball. She is sexy and dirty and does not give a damn.

In 2009, 19 years after Halston's death, the brand launched its 'Heritage' range, with all creations based on the designer's own archival sketches. This is where the company has enjoyed most success – as a straightforward evocation of the past. Several of these heritage pieces are featured in seventies-set crime drama *American Hustle* (2013), selected by costumier Michael Wilkinson.

Halston makes complete sense for the character of Sydney Prosser (Amy Adams): someone from humble beginnings who constantly reinvents herself; a con-woman to whom perception is everything. Most of Adams's costumes are body-hugging and revealing, reflecting her fragile yet divisive state of mind. If in doubt, show more. The actress has 36 outfit changes in the movie, a mix of high-end pieces from Halston, Gucci and Diane von Fürstenburg and custom ensembles. The fabrics are soft and sensual, and the lines dramatic. Halston allowed access to their archives when Wilkinson explained his manifesto for Sydney: sexy, strong, fashion forward. With the company's mixed fortunes over the years, they were only too pleased to have the Halston name re-energized on screen. Sydney's style comes to fruition as she matures into her role-within-a-role as English aristocrat Lady Edith Greensly. Even if Sydney herself never really understands what it means to come from money, she does comprehend the

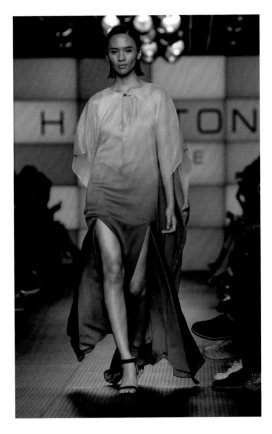

p90 Rene Russo wearing contemporary (and completely see-through) Halston for the dance scene in *The Thomas Crown Affair*

—

p91 left Spring/Summer 2015 Halston 'Heritage' show during Indonesia Fashion Week; this silk chiffon dress reinterprets the classic seventies-era Halston seen in *American Hustle*

—

p91 right Beige silk chiffon blouse worn by Amy Adams in *American Hustle*, one of four appearances of the brand (and the Halston 'Heritage' line) in the film

importance of image. This is the role of costume design: to echo the mind of a character within their setting.

Altogether there are four Halston appearances in *American Hustle*. During the opening sequence, Sydney wears a beige silk chiffon blouse combined with a genuine seventies belt and a suede skirt that Michael Wilkinson had made specially. Second, an eye-catching turquoise twist-front dress from Halston 'Heritage'. Third, a plunging beige knit top and hip-length camel coat, both vintage Halston, worn with a chocolate-brown silk jersey skirt suit by Giorgio Armani. Lastly, for the final con — and Wilkinson's personal favourite outfit — a Halston Heritage brown leather dress, paired with Gucci high-heel loafers and Gucci horsebit jewellery.

American Hustle alone would not be enough to reignite Halston's fire, which is still struggling to find its place as anything other than period curiosity. Even six 'Heritage' appearances in *Sex and the City* (TV show and movies), thanks to then Halston president and chief creative officer Sarah Jessica Parker, could not do that. However, the present does not affect Halston's legacy as, along with perhaps Yves Saint Laurent, the most important label of the seventies.

HARDY AMIES

THE GRASS IS GREENER (1960)
TWO FOR THE ROAD (1967)
2001: A SPACE ODYSSEY (1968)

Hardy Amies at work on a collection in 1952 with his fabric board in the background
—
p92 Hardy Amies designed gowns for Deborah Kerr in *The Grass Is Greener*. The film also featured costumes by Christian Dior for co-star Jean Simmons

The establishment's choice, staunch traditionalist and Queen Elizabeth's own personal dressmaker until his death in 2003, Sir Hardy Amies will forever be remembered as fashion's regal statesman. Amies was a shrewd businessman, having built a Savile Row tailoring business after World War II that sprang into an elegant house catering for the upper echelons of society. Nonetheless, unlike his customer base, who would consider self-promotion vulgar, Amies had no qualms about getting his name out there, particularly through cinema. He contributed to costumes on several films throughout the 1960s, including *The Amorous Mr Prawn* (1962), *The Alphabet Murders* (1965) and, most memorably, *2001: A Space Odyssey* (1968). Amies's first major motion picture was *Maytime in Mayfair* (1949), forming part of a *Vogue* magazine sequence for celebrated designers of the day. His double-breasted flared coat with huge wrapped collar-cum-scarf displays staggering workmanship.

Hardy Amies created a relaxed look for the well-heeled Englishman from the fifties onward: narrow-legged trousers, country check shirt (minus tie), and natural or dyed cashmere cardigan. While teenagers were experimenting with leather jackets and T-shirts, their fathers would be peering over a newspaper wearing the patented gentleman's uniform of Amies.

There is no clearer example of this look than on Albert Finney as Mark Wallace in *Two for the Road* (1967); next to his fashionista wife Joanna (Audrey Hepburn; see also pages 17, 144) Wallace, dressed by Hardy Amies, is every inch the unflappable don.

For *The Grass Is Greener* (1960), Amies was tasked with costuming Deborah Kerr, with Christian Dior dressing co-star Jean Simmons. Director Stanley Donan (*Singin' in the Rain*, *Funny Face*, *Charade*) often employed couture fashion to give his films a larger-than-life presence. *The Grass Is Greener* is an oddball comedy centring on Kerr's haughty housewife, Hilary, Countess of Rhyall, who begins a courtly affair with an American oil baron. The sedate attire for Hilary by Amies contrasts with noisy heiress Hattie Durant (Simmons). While Hilary sports a primly elegant royal blue dress with matching jacket, Hattie wears a bright orange signature Dior swing coat, featuring big buttons, big stand collar, big sleeves – big everything. Hilary is a straight-laced Englishwoman running wild for once in her life, although her grey trousers and light green sweater ensemble, with socks matching the sweater, feels most Hardy Amies. While certainly not mannish, it is inspired by the off-duty masculine silhouette of Amies. The only thing Hilary lacks is a hunting rifle slung over her shoulder.

There remains speculation as to why Stanley Kubrick chose Hardy Amies to costume civilian attire for *2001: A Space Odyssey* (1968), and because of the director's deeply personal methodology speculation is all it can be. The fact is, however, that Kubrick appreciated irony, and there is no greater irony than having a tailor infatuated with the establishment working alongside an auteur known for rallying against it. The outcome was genre-defining costume design that is not only relevant now, but wearable too.

Amies's costumes for *2001: A Space Odyssey* are first seen aboard the Pan Am space plane. Here, gentlemen's executive attire is a futuristic update on the classic lounge suit, with a comfortable nod to the late sixties. The suit is worn without a tie, as this would obviously be problematic in zero gravity, and with Velcro fastenings instead of buttons. Single-breasted, with a notch lapel and narrow vents, the jacket sports a clean chest and natural shoulders. Trousers are lean, but not tight, and cut to finish without a break; this latter detail dates the trousers to some degree, as nowadays pant hems generally rest on shoes. Colour is muted to befit hierarchical status (note a briefly glimpsed space station photographer in a loud check suit).

The first stewardess we see aboard the space plane (played by Heather Downham) wears a uniform of slim trousers with permanent crease, three-quarter-length-sleeve box jacket, slip-on 'grip shoes' and a bulbous helmet made by milliner Freddie Fox that functions as a safety or 'bump' hat. This overall look is unquestionably inspired by French designer André Courrèges's 'Moon Girl' collection from 1965 (see page 16). Hardy Amies is not necessarily remembered as a visionary, and his style is certainly more classically influenced than innovative, but he understood how to separate fad from modernism. The stewardess costumes of *2001: A Space Odyssey* constitute a paradox when viewed within a fashion-history cycle: they were influenced by André Courrèges, who was influenced by British designer John Bates, who was then influenced by Hardy Amies's costumes for the later episodes of *The Avengers* television series.

Trends during the sixties both originated from and inspired cinema. The science fiction genre was more popular than ever, and all eyes were on the future – something that was celebrated by the Russian edition of *Wallpaper* magazine, which paid homage to the female costumes in *2001: A Space Odyssey* with a limited-edition cover photo in November 2012. Hardy Amies, a man so associated with the old guard, created an avant-garde fashion aesthetic that still feels contemporary nearly 50 years later.

p94 top Dressed entirely in Hardy Amies, Albert Finney represented the utilitarian Brit abroad in *Two for the Road*, alongside Audrey Hepburn's increasingly fashion-forward wardrobe

—

p94 bottom Hardy Amies 'Street Style' collection for Spring/Summer 2016, a present-day update on Albert Finney's gentrified costumes in *Two for the Road*

—

p95 Minimalist stewardess costume by Hardy Amies for *2001: A Space Odyssey*. Amies's creations for the film are externally similar to those of designers John Bates, Pierre Cardin and André Courrèges

HELEN ROSE

FATHER OF THE BRIDE (1950)
CAT ON A HOT TIN ROOF (1955)
HIT THE DECK (1955)
THE SWAN (1956)

Helen Rose sketching at her board. Rose is known for creating some of the grandest and best-remembered wedding dresses of all time

—

p96 Later nicknamed 'The Cat', this Grecian-style white chiffon dress was made by Helen Rose for Elizabeth Taylor in *Cat on a Hot Tin Roof*

Born in 1904, Helen Rose began dressmaking in the cabarets and clubs of twenties Chicago. Though financially secure, she moved to Los Angeles and found work as a sketch artist. Twentieth Century Fox were the first to employ Rose in a costumier capacity, but it was not until joining Metro-Goldwyn-Mayer (MGM) in 1944 that her movie career really got underway. Eventually becoming head of costume after Irene Lentz, Rose stayed at the studio until 1966, winning two Academy Awards before leaving to set up her own fashion line, 'The House of Helen Rose'.

Rose's first onscreen credit was for dancers' costumes (a role she repeated often) for *In the Legion Now* (1936). *Ziegfeld Follies* (1946) was her first proper costume credit for MGM, and stands as one of the most indicative of her contribution to cinema. The film is essentially comprised of musical skits featuring Judy Garland and Lucille Ball with knowingly cartoonish, copiously feathered stage wear reflecting the peculiar fractured narrative.

The darling of many Hollywood stars, especially through the fifties and sixties, Rose is perhaps most closely associated with Grace Kelly. She designed four of Kelly's films while at MGM. They were an ideal team: Rose had a talent for creating understated elegance, and Kelly had a fondness for wearing it.

One of Rose's most famous costumes for Kelly was an ivory silk chiffon evening dress with lace flower appliqué in *The Swan* (1956), in which Kelly played a soon-to-be-married princess –reflecting Kelly's real life, as she was just about to marry Prince Rainier of Monaco. The film debuted in cinemas a week after the ceremony. Rose designed Kelly's wedding dress (actually two for separate parts of the service), something she had already done for another of her favourite collaborators, Elizabeth Taylor, in 1950.

Hit the Deck (1955) is all the Helen Rose you ever need. Far more varied than *Ziegfeld Follies* (1946) or even *On the Town* (1949), it runs the gamut of Rose's skills from performance costume to daywear to out-and-out evening showstoppers, all the while maintaining a naval uniform of bell-bottoms and serge jumpers for the male cast. The film is a typical musical revolving around sailors on shore leave, dancing, flirting and eventually hooking up with their girls in glorious Technicolor. Costume collector and Helen Rose aficionado Debbie Reynolds features throughout, but Jane Powell gets most attention as the effervescent Susan Smith. Her introduction wearing a teal fit-and-flare dress featuring white contrast club collar and white trim on the elbow-length sleeves, with red and white striped horizontal 'necktie' attachment, defines the Helen Rose look in a nutshell.

Rose designed elegant though largely unchallenging and 'safe' clothing; she championed good taste rather than creating it. Nonetheless, she loved adding a touch of fun to her garments with fabric or fanciful appliqué, such as Susan's necktie, which hints at the cheekiness in her personality. Her evening attire is once again the epitome of transitional Helen Rose: progressive but not revolutionary. Her backless red sequined halter-neck dress with full circle skirt and matching red sequined bolero jacket feels appropriate for the mid-fifties flounce silhouette, though it is not exaggerated enough to become overly dated. Rose's costumes, stage wear notwithstanding, were chic fashion pieces that could comfortably live beyond the screen – and in many cases they did.

If Rose and Grace Kelly were simpatico, then Rose and Elizabeth Taylor were the dream team. Their mutual admiration was based on complete trust in one another: Rose knew her slinky gowns and close-fitting, pared-down daywear would beautifully complement Taylor's curvy figure; Taylor knew Rose would never let her step out – in costume or in real life – looking anything less than spectacular. Spectacular does not necessarily mean showy, although this was certainly an off-screen trademark for Taylor during later years. Elizabeth Taylor was only 18 when she wore Helen Rose's spectacular ivory wedding gown for *Father of the Bride* (1950). It looked so good, Rose was commissioned to design Taylor's real-life wedding dress the same year. (MGM paid for both.) In creating the costumes for *Cat on*

Jane Powell (right) in a red sequined dress with matching bolero jacket designed by Helen Rose for *Hit the Deck*

Elizabeth Taylor wearing a Helen Rose wedding dress in *Father of the Bride* in 1950. Rose also designed a dress for Taylor's real-life wedding the same year

a Hot Tin Roof (1955), Rose created borderline minimalist attire that said a lot with very little, particularly in terms of styling. Taylor's best-known costume as Southern society girl Maggie was a white Grecian-style silk chiffon gown, later nicknamed 'The Cat', teamed with silvery pearl sandals. Maggie is stubborn and fiery; the dress actually softens her character to some degree, while refusing to hide her raw sensuality. The Cat was heavily copied in department stores after the film's release. Rose capitalized on it too, releasing a version under her own dress label.

Though costume design's primary responsibility today is to interpret character, Helen Rose comes from a time when the role of costume was almost solely to make movie stars look beautiful. Rose was not known for being historically accurate with her period clothing – her liberal use of chiffon regardless of the era being a good example – but she left her mark on cinema with painstaking attention to detail and a desire to incorporate, although never blindly recreate, era trends.

Grace Kelly as Princess Alexandra in *The Swan*. The silk chiffon evening gown by Rose sold at auction for $110,000 in 2011

HERMÈS

THE ROYAL TENENBAUMS (2001)
LE DIVORCE (2003)
THE PROPOSAL (2009)
WALL STREET: MONEY NEVER SLEEPS (2010)
BLUE JASMINE (2013)

Hermès shop window with handbag and scarves in Paris, 1947. By this point the brand had been trading for nearly 100 years

—

p100 Cate Blanchett's penniless character in *Blue Jasmine* holds onto her 'Birkin', believing that it, along with an increasingly grubby Chanel suit, defines her

For a brand that thrives on heritage, the Hermès name is generally a blink-and-miss-it moment in cinema. Hermès was originally established in Paris in 1837 as a harness manufacturer, but the brand really came to prominence in the first half of the twentieth century, making luxury accessories. Their intricately hand-crafted leather bags and silk scarves became part of French culture at a time when all the world respected Paris as the epitome of chic sophistication. Italy, New York and London have since shared that crown, though the caché of owning an Hermès handbag has not diminished. The presence of Hermès in film clearly signals a character who is wealthy, elite, somebody who knows somebody.

Most production budgets cannot stretch to purchasing Hermès, so it is down to enterprising costume designers to beg, steal or borrow whatever they need. For upper-middle-class comedy/dramas such as *Le Divorce* (2003) and *Blue Jasmine* (2013), the bag – for it practically always is a bag – represents the type of status even the wealthy cannot easily acquire. For example, no matter how much money you have, an Hermès 'Birkin' still has a rumoured four-year waiting list. The more difficult it is to procure an object of beauty, the more keenly we want it.

Despite their largely female fan base, Hermès still has a place in the affluent gentleman's wardrobe. Shia LaBeouf, as determined young broker Jacob Moore in *Wall Street: Money Never Sleeps* (2010), briefly sports an Hermès tie that was widely coveted on the film's release. It was a one-off, custom-made for costume designer Ellen Mirojnick.

The 'Birkin' carried by Gwyneth Paltrow as Margot Tenenbaum in *The Royal Tenenbaums* (2001) was almost certainly received as a gift from her mother, who flashes a newer version throughout the film. One-time child genius Margot is composed of an unswerving costume uniform constructed of famous brands: the Fendi fur coat, Lacoste tennis dress, 'Birkin' bag – these are all consistent facets of someone who cannot let go of their youthful zenith. She is a bourgeois hipster.

The bags featured in *Le Divorce* and *The Proposal* (2009) were borrowed from Hermès and a private collector respectively. Costume designer Carol Ramsey specifically needed a 'Kelly' for *Le Divorce* because it is mentioned by name in the source novel, though here the original colour is swapped for a red crocodile 'Kelly 28' (indicating the bag's length in centimetres). *Le Divorce* is a lavish tale focused on the contrasting love lives of two sisters in Paris. The 'Kelly' gifted to Kate Hudson's character Isabel is visible enough to be a member of the cast. During the finale this same bag is thrown from the Eiffel Tower as rejection of the status it symbolizes. Well, not the very same: Ramsey actually purchased a counterfeit 'stunt bag' for this scene. The real 'Kelly' was put under lock and key by Hermès every night of shooting.

In *The Proposal*, Sandra Bullock's anxious New York book editor Margaret arrives in Alaska wearing Christian Louboutin heels and an Hermès 'Birkin' over her arm. The 'Birkin', named after actress Jane Birkin is, to the trained eye, slightly larger than the 'Kelly', with two straps instead of one. Even though a 'Birkin' is intended as the more practical bag, its comically colossal size has the opposite effect for fish-out-of-water Margaret.

Cate Blanchett, as former socialite Jasmine in *Blue Jasmine*, had most of her designer wardrobe procured on loan by enterprising costumier Suzy Benzinger – including a 'Birkin', which would otherwise have been beyond Benzinger's $35,000 budget. Blanchett's cradles her 'Birkin' like a newborn baby – maybe not quite as gently (cringe as a handbag worth five figures is dropped unceremoniously next to a freeway), but no more keen for it to be taken away.

The Hermès bag is a symbol of Jasmine's feverish desire for acceptance in a bitchy, moneyed society that only remembers her name because she had it embossed on a set of Louis Vuitton luggage. For the kudos it buys, only an Hermès will do.

p102 top Shia LaBeouf wearing a custom-made Hermès necktie in *Wall Street: Money Never Sleeps*
—

p102 bottom The Hermès Birkin sported by Gwyneth Paltrow's sullen Margot in *The Royal Tenenbaums* is as integral to her fractured persona as the Fendi mink coat
—

p103 top Kate Hudson's Kelly bag for *Le Divorce* was loaned by Hermès. The one she tosses off the Eiffel Tower at the end of the film is (mercifully) a fake
—

p103 bottom The huge Hermès Birkin owned by Sandra Bullock's character Margaret in *The Proposal* was actually borrowed from a private collector in order to meet the film's strict costume budget

HOWARD GREER

THE TEN COMMANDMENTS (1923)
BRINGING UP BABY (1938)
CAREFREE (1938)

This 1938 Howard Greer costume sketch for *Carefree* displays pronounced, rather forties-era shoulders

—

p104 All Katharine Hepburn's costumes for *Bringing Up Baby*, including this gold lamé dress and wacky 'cosmic veil', were designed by Howard Greer

As a young sketch artist, Howard Greer got his break with the fashion house Lucile, among the flounce and cascading fabric of the Edwardian period. Lucile was owned by Lucy Christiana, Lady Duff Gordon, largely forgotten in bios of fashion greats, but a gifted couturière and astute businesswoman who pioneered the industry, opening stores in New York, London, Chicago and Paris. Lady Duff Gordon also made costumes for several films during the silent era. Greer learned his craft with Lady Duff Gordon before leaving to work in the movie industry himself. After a successful stint as a costume designer in Hollywood, he returned to fashion until his retirement.

Greer was employed as a sketch artist in the Famous Players-Lasky Corporation, although not in Cecil B. DeMille's own subdivision of the company. Greer did, however, work (uncredited) with DeMille and Claire West, one of the first contracted female costume designers ever, on *The Ten Commandments* (1923). Greer later became head of the costume department for Famous Players-Lasky, which, by the time he left in 1927, had morphed into Paramount Pictures. During his stint at Lasky-Paramount, Greer took a young, aspiring prospect under his wing and taught her how to draw. We can thank Howard Greer, at least in part, for giving us legendary costume designer Edith Head.

One of Howard Greer's best-remembered films, *Christopher Strong* (1933), required his teaming up with RKO head designer Walter Plunkett. Although Greer created most of Katharine Hepburn's tailored clothing as aviator Lady Cynthia Darrington, he did not make the silver 'moth dress' she wears for a fancy-dress party – that was all Plunkett. Greer would work with Hepburn again, however, on possibly her most celebrated movie, the screwball comedy *Bringing Up Baby* in 1938.

In *Carefree* (1938), Howard Greer playfully demonstrates that clothes designed for film can continue to influence – acknowledged or otherwise – contemporary fashion many decades later. In this typically light Fred and Ginger farce, Ginger Rogers plays Amanda Cooper, a radio singer who falls for her fiancé's friend, Dr Tony Flagg (Astaire). After dreaming about Flagg, Amanda arrives for her psychiatry session wearing a dark short-sleeve dress with padded shoulders, featuring a tea-length skirt, narrow patent belt, wide-brim floppy hat (she has lots of these), mink stole and black high-heel shoes. The bodice front of her dress exhibits a charming felt appliqué heart motif with arrows directed toward it; the subtext being that these are Cupid's golden arrows flying straight at her heart. Amanda is visiting Flagg to interpret her unconscious mind, but the reason for her problems – love – is staring him in the face. The costume has inspired a number of fashion interpretations. In 1947, Susan Dannenburg's 'Jezebel' sweater referenced Greer's creation, featuring a solitary dagger struck through a bleeding heart. Karen Walker in her Autumn/Winter 2007/8 show took Greer's overall silhouette (though with a shorter skirt) and appliqué but substituted lightning bolts for arrows. Most recently Marco Zanini for Schiaparelli paid homage to Greer's original costume, and the 'Jezebel' sweater, with a punky design of arrows shooting toward a bleeding heart.

Even though it might not seem so on the surface, *Bringing Up Baby* (1938) is very much a costume movie. Though neither outlandish science fiction nor period drama, the film uses clothes as part of the narrative, frequently with comedic intent. At this point in her career, Katharine Hepburn was still establishing her 'look' of relaxed easy wear based on the unrestricted comfort of traditionally masculine dress. Trousers in a wide-leg twenties 'Oxford Bag' cut became Hepburn's trademark style. She wears trousers in *Bringing Up Baby*, though most of her clothes echo a late-thirties vogue for stately proportioned, less fluid shapes. Most important is a dress her character Susan Vance chooses for evening drinks at a posh restaurant. At the end of the sequence, she rejects the garment by accidentally tearing a strip off the seat, revealing her underwear – perhaps a subtle comment by Greer on Hepburn's unsuitability for the gown's rigid silhouette. The dress, very tightly fitted, floor length, finished in gold lamé with squared shoulders, is a bizarre choice

for Hepburn's willowy figure. The bobbing cosmic veil encircling her head further implies this dress is high fashion of the era played for laughs.

Whether or not Greer's gowns were intended to live beyond the screen, paper-pattern company Butterick still offered several of Greer's designs as part of their 'Starred' collection. 'Hollywood Patterns', which unlike the Butterick versions ran successfully for 15 years from 1932, were presented as 'inspired by' the film dresses as opposed to direct copies. By this point, Greer had left Paramount to open his own boutique, Greer Inc., making high-end couture clothing in the vein, if not style, of his mentor Lady Duff Gordon. Greer continued to design for film on a freelance basis while running Greer Inc. In 1946 he introduced a lucrative ready-to-wear line, showcasing his sustained preference for majestic evening and occasion wear.

With *The French Line* (1953), Greer once more collaborated with a fellow costume designer, this time Michael Woulfe; both created gowns for star Jane Russell as heiress Mary 'Mame' Carson. Exactly who made the film's most sensational costume, a satin jewel-beaded cut-out bathing suit worn with opera gloves during the 'Lookin' for Trouble' dance sequence, is unclear. Woulfe certainly drew the garment sketches but may not have been directly responsible for creating the suit. Producer Howard Hughes had a considerable hand in the proceedings, requesting that the costume be ever lower and the cutouts more pronounced, until Russell was more nude than clothed. Censors were outraged, and for the movie's second release Hughes made considerable edits to the 'Lookin' for Trouble' sequence in order to secure certification. *The French Line* was Howard Greer's last credited film as costumier, but he continued to design full time for Greer Inc. until retiring in 1962.

p106 Cecil B. DeMille's *The Ten Commandments*. Howard Greer was joint costume designer for the film but, typical for freelance designers of the time, uncredited for the role

—

p107 top Ginger Rogers's cupid-motif dress for *Carefree*. This dress would have a legacy in fashion decades on. Howard Greer is credited alongside costume designer Edward Stevenson for his contribution to the film

—

p107 bottom Marco Zanini's second collection for Schiaparelli in 2014 gave more than a fleeting glance toward *Carefree* with his vampy hearts and arrows dress

HUBERT DE GIVENCHY

SABRINA (1954)
BONJOUR TRISTESSE (1958)
BREAKFAST AT TIFFANY'S (1961)
CHARADE (1963)
HOW TO STEAL A MILLION (1966)
MOONRAKER (1979)

Hubert de Givenchy with Audrey Hepburn in his Paris workshop, 1991

—

p108 Classically styled Audrey Hepburn wearing Givenchy for *Sabrina*, their first onscreen project together

While it is not fair, or accurate, to claim Hubert de Givenchy was defined by Audrey Hepburn, their extraordinary bond as designer and muse was essential in forging both careers. Their working lives were completely intertwined.

Hepburn met Givenchy in 1953, when she was just 22 years old. Signed to star in *Sabrina*, she was sent by director Billy Wilder to meet the up-and-coming couturier and select costumes for the 'after' makeover of her character. Official costume designer for the film Edith Head was passed over, openly disappointed at being left with the 'before' portion of Hepburn's wardrobe. Her chance to shine in the world of fashion was handed over to an actual Paris designer. As the well-told story goes, Givenchy was expecting the far more famous Katharine Hepburn, not Audrey. When the fresh-faced actress arrived in slim pants and flat shoes, he was reputedly amused but far from convinced. Warming to Audrey's natural charm, Givenchy gave her samples from his previous year's Spring/Summer collection. The transformation was astounding – from thin, wide-eyed hopeful to chic Paris darling. His little black dress (LBD) sold the collaboration and would continue to symbolize the pair's harmonious and co-dependent relationship over the next 40 years.

Hubert de Givenchy was mentored by Cristóbal Balenciaga, so it stands to reason they both shared a love of simplicity. Givenchy's first collection was an innovative mix of eveningwear separates that set the benchmark for his career. Despite their exclusiveness, his clothes were designed to be comfortable. Givenchy skimmed form instead of creating it. His clothes fitted the figure, but not always *on* the figure. This is why the Hepburn association made so much sense.

The most famous Givenchy/Hepburn collaboration is often the most incorrectly reported. Unlike most of Hepburn's later projects, her costumes for *Breakfast at Tiffany's* (1961) were not exclusively by her favourite designer. The film was actually costumed by Edith Head. There are three black dresses worn by Hepburn as Holly Golightly, though only one was designed by Givenchy, and even that was remade by Head. Givenchy's LBD (more of a long black dress in reality), as seen during the opening credits, was considered too racy, with its lengthy leg slit (similar to that featured on the poster art). Head completely redesigned the skirt and added small weights to the hem so it hung evenly. She copied the top half of Givenchy's original almost exactly, then accessorized with Tiffany diamonds, a pearl necklace and long black gloves. Consequently, the version shown in the film is not Givenchy's but Head's interpretation based on his design.

p 110 top Edith Head's copy of Givenchy's rejected black dress for *Breakfast at Tiffany's*. The top half of the dress is almost identical to Givenchy's original, just accessorized with Tiffany diamonds and a pearl necklace
—

p 110 bottom left Givenchy Spring/Summer 2015 show during Paris Fashion Week. The little black dress lives on and on
—

p 110 bottom right Sketch by Edith Head of Givenchy's black dress for *Breakfast at Tiffany's*. Head reworked the original dress, though its initial incarnation can be seen in the poster art for the film
—

p 111 left The Givenchy woollen coat in *Charade*, recreated in yellow for the film from original black featured in the designer's own 1962 Autumn/Winter collection
—

p 111 right Red for danger, animal print for wildness: Hepburn in top-to-toe Givenchy for *Charade*

Three identical dresses were provided by Givenchy, although only Head's incarnation appears in the finished movie. This did not stop Christie's auction house selling one example for almost half a million pounds in 2006, despite its not seeing a second of screen time. The *Breakfast at Tiffany's* LBD myth has fuelled itself over time, which ironically was counter-productive for Givenchy as he produced far more fun and interesting work for Hepburn throughout the sixties.

Charade (1963) is the consummate Givenchy/Hepburn collaboration. The breezy spy caper, co-starring Cary Grant, was directed by Stanley Donen, who would go on to make Hepburn's most important fashion film *not* featuring Givenchy, *Two for the Road* (1967; see pages 17, 144). In *Charade* Hepburn plays 'Reggie' Lampert, a stylish transatlantic caught in a preposterous web of deception. Givenchy provided all of Hepburn's ensembles. Reggie's looks are sophisti-cated and larger than life – aspirational rather than relatable – but then *Charade* was not claiming to be realistic. Even in context, Reggie's upscale ensembles make no sense. On her return from the Alps, Reggie is left with only a Lufthansa flight bag, yet changes from one outfit to another practically on the turn of a scene, from a three-quarter-sleeve red woollen coat (the colour stressing Reggie's imminent peril) and

Audrey Hepburn in costume for *How to Steal a Million*.
Givenchy embraced the space-age vibe of André Courrèges

Givenchy provided Deborah Kerr's hats and formal wear
for *Bonjour Tristesse*

All of Lois Chiles's costumes for the James Bond film
Moonraker were designed by Givenchy

leopard-print cloche-style hat (not a pillbox because
the crown is domed) to a two-piece wool crepe black
skirt suit trimmed in imitation jet and lined in silk.
Hepburn appealed to both female audiences, who
wanted her clothes, and male audiences, who wanted
her. She lacked the coolness of a Paris fashionista. In
terms of style, Hepburn's costumes were not radical,
leaning on the previous decade's swing silhouette, similar to Nina Ricci's output at the time. However, that was
all set to change with her next outing; Givenchy truly
found the sixties with *How to Steal a Million* (1966).

Undoubtedly best remembered for Hepburn's
opening ensemble of white felt helmet hat with chin
strap, white plastic 'bug eye' sunglasses and off-white
dress with matching jacket, *How to Steal a Million* is
more tongue-in-cheek with regards to costume than
Charade. This first outfit was a nod to the popular
space-age trend exploding around Europe, and André
Courrèges's first 'Moon Girl' collection (see page 16),
although Hepburn's hat strap is tied and the Courrèges
version was not, and her low-heel shoes differ from
the flat kid 'Go-Go' boots of Courrèges. The sunglasses
are by Oliver Goldsmith, but the dress and jacket are
pure Givenchy.

Charade made no reference to the perfection
of Reggie's wardrobe, whereas Hepburn's character in
How to Steal a Million, Nicole Bonnet, is deconstructed

at every available opportunity. Whether wearing a pink
woollen coat with lacy chiffon nightdress and PVC
wellington boots, or a black lace dress with matching
face mask in a crowded restaurant, Nicole is acknowledged as looking a bit silly. But the point is she does
not care. The face mask is actually a costume within
a costume, as she attempts to secure the services of
bemused gentleman thief Simon Dermott (Peter O'Toole).
Rather than actually committing a burglary dressed in a
couture stripy jumper with a bag labelled 'swag' over her
shoulder, Nicole is told by Simon to 'give Givenchy the
night off' and wear a frumpy cleaner's uniform instead.
This knowing line is amusing as repartee but highlights
just how much of a walking mannequin Hepburn had
become for Givenchy. They both needed the space apart
that *Two for the Road* the following year would afford.

Hubert de Givenchy did not design solely for
Audrey Hepburn on screen; he provided hats and formal
wear for Deborah Kerr in *Bonjour Tristesse* (1958) and,
three decades on, Bond girl Lois Chiles in *Moonraker*
(1979), including a beautifully cut and absolutely
relevant black jumpsuit. The man himself retired from
design in 1995, although the company continues today
with a roll call of talent passing through its gates as
creative directors. On screen, however, Hepburn will
always be Givenchy's gift. She was, and remains, the
poster girl for fashion in cinema.

IRENE LENTZ

TO BE OR NOT TO BE (1942)
MIDNIGHT LACE (1960)
THE TOURIST (2010)

Irene Gibbons making research sketches in the Picture
Collection of the New York Public Library, 1944

—

p114 Bias-cut gown on Carole Lombard in *To Be or Not
to Be*. If there is one thing Irene will be remembered for,
it is cutting on the bias

Sharp tailored suits, inverted narrow-pleat skirts, wide-leg trousers and Grecian gowns on the bias, always cut, sewn and finished to perfection: these are the hallmarks of Irene Lentz. Her contribution to fashion and costume is throwback to a bygone era when, above all else, quality mattered. Quality was the style.

Born in 1900, Irene Lentz Gibbons, known professionally as Irene, studied dressmaking before moving from her home in Montana to open a small dress shop, Irene of California on the University of California campus in Los Angeles. Then she left to travel Europe, before returning to LA to open another boutique on Sunset Boulevard. This is where Irene established her name, thriving among the great and the good of celebrity culture. In 1935, luxury art deco department store Bullocks Wilshire even created a custom salon for Irene, which can still be visited today (although the store no longer trades), adorned with her garment sketches. The salon is testament to a bygone time when any woman with enough money could buy an original 'Irene exclusively for Bullocks Wilshire', directly overseen by the designer herself.

Irene's first movie break came when loyal customer Dolores del Río asked her to make gowns for *Flying Down to Rio* (1933) alongside RKO chief designer Walter Plunkett. Irene began freelancing, dressing the likes of Ginger Rogers, Hedy Lamarr and Ingrid Bergman, before in 1942 Metro-Goldwyn-Mayer (MGM) offered her the role of Executive Director in Charge of Costume, replacing Gilbert Adrian. She stayed in the position for eight years – contributing to *National Velvet* (1944), *The Postman Always Rings Twice* (1946) and *Easter Parade* (1948), among others – though her tenure was marked by difficult cost-cutting. The sartorial opulence of the thirties had passed, and studios were less inclined to spend money on extravagant costumes. Irene was often partnered with another designer; even in the top job she was a dressmaker first, costumier second. Alas, designing for movies meant she had to close her boutique and salon at Bullocks. When Irene left MGM she introduced Irene Inc. once again, this time at a more mass-market level. Very few compromises were made, and she continued to garner rave reviews throughout the rest of her career.

Irene's name was the icing on the cake for Carole Lombard when she came on board *To Be or Not to Be* (1942), and she finally had the opportunity to work with her favourite director, Ernst Lubitsch. Lombard never looked better: slinky gowns cut on the bias (so much bias) with scant, cleverly positioned appliqué, gave her a most glamorous swansong. She died in an air accident just one month before the film was released.

Doris Day's look of sophisticated yet functional attire was not Irene's creation; Jean Louis, who dressed Day in *Pillow Talk* (1959), was arguably the most influential costumier for her pillbox hats and tailored sheaths with matching coat ensembles. Day did, however, choose an Irene bateau-neck gown for the premiere of *Pillow Talk*. Irene honed the Jean Louis silhouette, redefined from all-out glamour to just accessibly rich. The consummate Irene/Day collaboration was *Midnight Lace* (1960), though it is not one of the actress's best-known pictures today, possibly because it was a thriller not a comedy. Nonetheless, it was intended as a showcase for Irene, with Day only too happy to play model for her friend. *Midnight Lace* was promoted with a six-minute featurette sent out in advance to cinemas. With Irene herself introducing the costumes and Day modelling, this was basically an advertisement for every item of clothing Day wears in the movie. These ensembles were all individually numbered, such as No. 1900-Ex2, a lambswool swing coat with fur funnel neck, interior fur-trimmed three-quarter-length sleeves and matching leather gloves, which Day as woman-in-peril Kit Preston sports in the film's opening scene. Patrons could take the garment numbers to the nearest department store carrying Irene Inc. and purchase off the rack.

Oddly, in the context of the story Kit actually buys her clothes from 'Hartnell's' in London (where the film is set), which presumably means fashion designer Norman Hartnell. If name-checking Irene was a promo too far, then it hardly mattered. Her signature touches

of outsized and atypical buttons, slash necklines for gowns and outfits of matching dresses and coats are all present. Day's best-remembered costume is referenced early in the story. Kit displays for her husband what appears to be a black lace negligée (he refers to it as a 'thingummy'); later the garment is revealed to be one-piece suit with cropped legs and attached cape. An odd choice for a romantic tryst, and even more so for Irene and her generally undemanding feminine aesthetic, but all becomes clear when Kit is chased out of her top-floor apartment onto scaffolding erected on the building site next door. Kit has to clamber and climb, swinging her body and legs in all manner of angles in front of the camera, before finally descending a ladder to the ground. Obviously she could not have done this in a negligee – and neither could Day (or her stunt double). Costume and fashion can co-exist, even in a blatant marketing ploy like the one for *Midnight Lace*, but the needs of costume must be served first. What seems a somewhat out-of-place garment in the fashion featurette makes sense in the movie itself. Irene's work did not go unrewarded, as she snagged an Academy Award nomination for Best Costume Design (Colour) – unusual for a contemporary with characters in 'normal' attire.

Sadly, Irene committed suicide in 1962, aged 61. But her look is more relevant now than ever as representation of ageless elegance. Little dates Irene. Costume designer Colleen Atwood created the look for

Angelina Jolie's well-heeled femme fatale Elise Clifton-Ward in *The Tourist* (2010) using Irene's classic silhouette. She even based one signature piece, her off-white silk sheath dress on a vintage Irene design, adding some personal panache in the form of mocha cashmere wrap and suede gloves – a very Irene touch.

In 2013, Greg LaVoi, costume designer for television series *The Closer* (2005–12), relaunched the Irene name as a contemporary update on her timeless designs – a celebration of Irene's chic made-in-America craftsmanship and neat, slender silhouette. This is not Paris; Irene is the 'California look'. LaVoi has more than 300 vintage Irene dresses in his own personal collection, which he often used for Kyra Sedgwick's character Brenda Leigh Johnson on *The Closer*.

Though Irene's life was cut short, her legacy in cinema and fashion is embedded in history.

JEAN LOUIS

GILDA (1946)

THE SOLID GOLD CADILLAC (1956)

THOROUGHLY MODERN MILLIE (1967)

Jean Louis during his time at Columbia Pictures, surrounded by Hollywood beauties, 1944

—

p118 Rita Hayworth in *Gilda,* wearing one of the most famous dresses in cinema history, designed by Jean Louis as the epitome of unconstrained sexuality

Starting his career as a fashion designer, Jean Louis became technically proficient at creating works of costume wizardry. He made women look like perfume bottles: tall and lean, yet somehow curvy. One of Louis's best-known costumes was for Rita Hayworth in *Gilda* (1946). The gown, which had to be strapless so Hayworth could move and undress, was constructed of black satin, cut as an incredibly tight sheath to announce Gilda as the ultimate embodiment of sexual desire. Louis had to create an impossible frame on the already slim Hayworth. He made a harness and corset to suppress her waist (she had recently given birth) and lift up her breasts, with the top of the skirt encased in a soft plastic to retain shape. It was a costume in the purest sense, suitable only for its purpose.

Born in Paris in 1907, Jean Louis was employed by haute couture house Agnés as a sketch artist before moving to New York in 1936 to design for Hattie Carnegie, best known for its trendsetting nipped-in 'Carnegie suit'. Hattie Carnegie was already importing gowns from Paris at the time, so Jean Louis made perfect sense at the upscale boutique. Joan Cohen, wife of Columbia Pictures studio head Harry Cohen, herself a stylish Manhattanite, persuaded Louis to come work for her husband designing costumes. In 1944, Louis joined Columbia as assistant to Travis Banton. Louis had been

colleagues with Banton at Hattie Carnegie, though Banton was now a mentor to Louis. When Banton moved on from Columbia, Jean Louis took over as head of costume. His first film piece was for his long-time friend Irene Dunne in *Together Again* (1944).

In 1958 Louis moved to Universal, hitting his stride with the studio's glossy and highly successful Doris Day/Rock Hudson comedies. It was Louis who transformed Day from the all-American girl next door to chic and sexy glamour puss – and *Pillow Talk* (1959) was the perfect vehicle. Basically a mild sex comedy, *Pillow Talk* features Day as happily unattached interior designer Jan Morrow, who falls for laidback songwriter Brad Allen (Hudson). Bill Thomas was overall costumier for the film, while Louis retained his usual 'gowns by' credit for Day. There is conscious effort here to 'sex up' Day for the soon-to-be-swinging sixties. However, this is late-fifties New York, not London, favouring shape rather than form, fur rather than PVC, flounce rather than a spare silhouette. Louis's look is a purposely uniform collection of sheath dresses wrapped in heavy silk satin coats and brimless hats. Occasionally the new decade of exotic prints against bold block colour intrudes, such as Jan's bright red unstructured coat with three-quarter-length sleeves and matching button closure, red suit with just-below-the-knee pencil skirt and tall leopard-skin cloche hat with flat crown,

leopard-skin hand-warmer and tan high-heel shoes. *Pillow Talk* gave us a new Day, thanks in no small part to Louis, who became a favourite go-to costume and fashion designer for the actress.

For *Thoroughly Modern Millie* (1967), set in 1922, the story of Millie Dillmount (Julie Andrews), a fresh-faced stenographer who moves to New York to be a 'modern' in search of love and a career, Jean Louis really pushed the boat out. This was a time when a renowned costumier's name still meant something. Universal were so excited about the film's fashion appeal they even produced a featurette, 'A Thoroughly Modern Wardrobe', to showcase the costumes worn by Andrews and co-stars Mary Tyler Moore as Miss Dorothy Brown and Carol Channing as Muzzy Van Hossmere. It covers virtually all of the outfits each actress wears, some might say, pedantic detail, right down to fabric and finish.

In the movie, Louis focuses his costumes on the three signature looks sported by Andrews's flapper, Moore's cute and classic lamb, and Channing's outrageous glamour queen. Millie's trademark ensemble is a shift dress, rudimentary at first, in thin grey wool with a pocketed waistband to which she alternates the trim. Then she moves to the black-and-white satin crepe with zigzag pattern, matching felt hat and black silk and red rose scarf and cream low-heel pointed-toe shoes to 'vamp' her boss – a natural sartorial evolution

that suits her go-getting, motivated character. Prim Miss Dorothy loosens up from a plush ice-blue satin dress with white net skirt swathed in blue rose petals and diamond-buckle shoes, to striking black lace over nude dress with floral accessory and black steel buckle. Muzzy's ensembles are the most fun. Millie might be the flapper in story terms, but growing-old-disgracefully Muzzy acts more like one. A hat of bleached-white vulture feathers, white speckled silk dress, huge emerald neck- lace and bracelet is her norm, along with a remarkable tea gown made from white silk crepe, huge bell sleeves trimmed in curled ostrich feathers, rope belt weighted with diamond tiers and a diamond choker to match. Jean Louis's efforts saw him nominated for an Oscar.

After being nominated for 14 Academy Awards (including colour and black-and-white categories before the two were combined), and winning once for *The Solid Gold Cadillac* (1956), Jean Louis decided to return full time to the world of fashion, launching his own ready-to-wear label Jean Louis Inc. in high-end department stores while continuing to costume free- lance for cinema. Louis was an all-rounder, as proficient at costume as he was at fashion. What he managed best throughout his extraordinary career, like so few others, was the seamless combination of both: clothes to watch, clothes to wear.

JEAN PAUL GAULTIER

KIKA (1993)

THE FIFTH ELEMENT (1997)

THE SKIN I LIVE IN (2011)

Jean Paul Gaultier in his signature stripes and 'man-skirt'

—

p122 Victoria Abril as 'Andrea Scarface' in *Kika*, wearing a stage costume designed by Jean Paul Gaultier

Jean Paul Gaultier is a fashion designer; it is his day job, so to speak. Yet his work for cinema has been so memorable that it almost outshines anything he has yet sent down a catwalk. His costume collaborations are sometimes award winning, and often outrageous, comments on clothing as a statement of character. Gaultier is influenced by the world around him: nature, architecture, people and art. Even his trademark stripes were inspired by a love of cartoon *Popeye the Sailor*. This motif in particular is one he has carried into film costume. Miette's (Judith Vittet) red striped sweater in *The City of Lost Children (La cité des enfants perdus*, 1995) is unmistakably Gaultier. Moreover, she inhabits a dreamscape marked with his visible nametag. Gaultier is the undisputed master of retaining a signature look on screen.

Amazingly, Gaultier has no formal training in the world of fashion, making his way into the industry through pure doggedness. As a teenager, Gaultier contacted Pierre Cardin with a collection of garment sketches and was immediately hired by the designer as his assistant. Gaultier, like fellow big-name designers Bill Blass and Roy Halston, is the personality behind the brand; he understands the need to be 'out there'. Although he launched his first collection in 1976, it was not until the eighties and nineties that Gaultier really

Costume designed by Jean Paul Gaultier for Madonna's 1990
Blonde Ambition tour, including conical bras for her and her
male backing dancers

Rhianna at the 2009 American Music Awards wearing
Gaultier reminiscent of Milla Jovovich's bandage costume
in *The Fifth Element*

hit. Along with matelot stripes, he also promoted more eccentric fads such as the 'man-skirt', and the 'cone' bra, as sported by Madonna during her 1990 Blonde Ambition tour. Gaultier does not see himself as a menswear or womenswear designer. He ignores gender constructs – what it means to be masculine or feminine – in favour of dressing the body only. What his clothes say about you is for you to decide.

This perception of shifting identity is readily apparent in the costumes Gaultier created for Victoria Abril as Andrea, aka 'Andrea Scarface', in *Kika* (1993). Director Pedro Almodóvar wanted glamour as catastrophe from the designer. Andrea's first outfit is a costume within a costume, a show-stopping sensationalist dress that she wears as host of an exploitation television show: a black velvet gown with slashed fishtail hem, long sleeves and feathered cuffs, covered in dripped red plastic to represent blood pouring from a burst chest area that reveals two fake breasts. The exposed breasts make this garment inherently outrageous while echoing her modus operandi for exposing shocking truth. Andrea's second show costume – a red-and-black PVC and bandage dress worn for her 'Bloody Ceremonies' segment – continues Gaultier's theme with a vision of thirties Hollywood rinsed through the mind of a contemporary surrealist. Away from her show, Andrea moves

from monstrous to practical, wearing a boiler-suit refashioned as a sartorial news van. Andrea's breasts are covered by two lamps and protective bull bars, while a bulky camera sits atop her head on a helmet. Again, Gaultier concentrates on the chest area, harking back to his fondness for underwear as outerwear and the perversion of everyday garments. Most amusing, and most Gaultier, is Andrea's 'truth' attire. Not grotesque or awkwardly functional but what she wears to meet an ex-lover in cafe – a basic striped sweater and waistcoat. Despite Kika's loudly proclaimed theme of (the compulsion of) voyeurism, this brief glimpse of Andrea away from the real-life victims she chooses to exploit actually feels most voyeuristic of all.

Most of Gaultier's work as a costume designer is for European and/or arthouse filmmakers. Director Peter Greenaway hired him as sole costumier for *The Cook, the Thief, His Wife and Her Lover* (1989). Gaultier was tasked with making clothes that changed through seven specific colour shades as characters passed from one set to another. It was as much of an experiment as the movie itself, mirroring Gaultier's own erratic and unpredictable approach to fashion.

Arguably Gaultier's most famous costumes to date are for science-fiction thriller *The Fifth Element* (1997). Comparatively inexperienced at the time,

Milla Jovovich in *The Fifth Element*. Gaultier's work shows
the influence of wrapped, bondage-style garments

Gaultier was a risk, hired only at director Luc Besson's insistence. Though the film was harshly reviewed at the time of release, it now has a cult following that embraces its overblown campness.

The Fifth Element is a fantasy set in the twenty-third century. Gaultier took his cue from Besson and approached the film as a recognizable progression of our own reality. Familiar elements from the designer are scattered throughout, such as a conical hat on trainee priest David (Charlie Creed-Miles) and thermal bandage as bondage attire on Leeloo (Milla Jovovich) – even the reverse of Korben Dallas's (Bruce Willis) orange singlet has bandage strapping. And, of course stripes, as seen on ship's steward Fog (Lee Evans). Willis was not happy about wearing the vest, apparently missing the day-glo wink to his famous costume from Die Hard (1988).

The most 'Gaultier' character in The Fifth Element is shock DJ Ruby Rhod (Chris Tucker), introduced wearing an off-the-shoulder leopardskin body-suit with attached boots and matching cape. By donning what could traditionally be defined as 'women's' clothes, Rhod splits his gender make-up in half. Most significant is that Rhod's ensembles do not denote his sexual orientation. Outwardly effeminate, interpretable as homosexual, he molests a skimpily dressed female steward, the scene edited in such a way that it was clearly something Besson wanted us to register.

Gaultier's sense of humour permeates wherever it can. The light tone allows us step back and
applaud its absurdity. A red-and-yellow Spandex
McDonald's uniform sported by fifties-esque diner
girls at a drive-thru, complete with golden arches motif,
is a riposte to the film's many incidences of product
placement. Fashion house Moschino released similarly
themed garments for their Autumn/Winter 2014 collection – swapping out the McDonald's arches for their
own Moschino 'M'.

If *The Fifth Element* is Jean Paul Gaultier's
most incredible contribution to costume, teaming up
with director Pedro Almodóvar for *The Skin I Live In*
(*La piel que habito*, 2011) is his most rational. Gaultier
collaborated with costumier Paco Delgado to make a
second-skin bodysuit for the character of Vera Cruz
(Elena Anaya), a man (now woman) healing after
forced sex-reassignment surgery. Almodóvar rejected
Gaultier's early sketches as too theatrical, perhaps
demonstrating that the designer works best within firm
boundaries – someone with a foothold on narrative
above all else. The stitching on Vera's bodysuit is a nod
to the scars healing on her body. Gaultier gets a chance
to be Gaultier, though, with a tiger suit that appears
later in the story, when a man rapes Vera. It is a risky
scene, ridiculous and disconcertingly amusing – all
facets of Jean Paul Gaultier and his life's work.

KARL LAGERFELD

BABETTE'S FEAST (1987)
HIGH HEELS (1991)
BROKEN EMBRACES (2009)

Karl Lagerfeld in 1972. A decade later he would take over and revitalize the house of Chanel

—

p128 Spring/Summer 1992 Chanel crepe sheath, as worn by Penélope Cruz in *Broken Embraces*

Karl Lagerfeld has reinvented form and style in every house he has worked for; he was fashion's tireless innovator. Lagerfeld began his career with Pierre Balmain, then later Jean Patou, Tiziani of Rome, Chloé and furs for Fendi, finally – his biggest coup – taking over at Chanel in 1983. He also releases several collections under his own name. Amazingly, Lagerfeld still found time for cinema, having directed three fashion shorts for Chanel, two of which feature founder Coco as the central character. Karl Lagerfeld was everywhere, yet somehow not ubiquitous.

Lagerfeld on screen is principally via Chanel, but there are early glimpses under his own guise. He exclusively dressed Janine Reynaud as exotic nightclub performer/murderous disciple of Satan Lorna Green in *Succubus* (*Necronomicon – Geträumte Sünden*, 1968). Lagerfeld was not to be pigeonholed, even back then, with Lorna's ensembles ranging from a clinically white trouser suit to Lurex silver shift with plastic disc strap inserts. His most sensational costume is a full-length red robe with long flared sleeves, tied at the waist and cut deep at the neckline. The skirt swells behind Lorna as she strides, occasionally exposing her plain black underwear. A rich shade of blood, this gown is Lorna's attire as she transitions into the satanic. She is referred to as 'the devil on earth', a title befitting her vamp-like make-up and overt costuming (as to be expected from director Jesús Franco, this is not a subtle movie).

Lagerfeld contributed to a handful of features during the seventies, including thriller *Ten Days' Wonder* (*La décade prodigieuse*, 1971), starring Orson Welles. He also made costumes for Stéphane Audran three times – most notably in Danish drama *Babette's Feast* (*Babettes Gæstebud*, 1987). Under the instruction of director Gabriel Axel, Lagerfeld designed for Audran a markedly plain refugee robe, deliberately Parisian in style, which was intended to set her apart from the rest of the cast. This was not a personal request of Audran, but an intentional differentiation for her character, mysterious and adept culinary artist Babette.

Pedro Almodóvar, a Spanish film-maker acutely aware of the character insight attainable through designer clothing, asked Karl Lagerfeld, a personal friend, to provide Victoria Abril's costumes for *High Heels* (*Tacones lejanos*, 1991). As news anchor-woman Rebeca, Abril wears Chanel almost entirely throughout. Rebeca has created a fragile facade in the shadow of her successful actress mother Becky del Páramo, who abandoned her as a child. At the beginning of the story, Becky, a tentatively remorseful diva, returns to her daughter after 15 years apart. Almodóvar drowns Rebeca in a white bouclé Chanel skirt suit with scalloped edging and gold buttons as she waits nervously at the airport. He purposely frames the 'CC' logo on Rebeca's sunglasses and the label inside her quilted '2.55' handbag. Soon after they meet, Becky comments with genuine enthusiasm, 'That Chanel really suits you.' And who could miss it? Rebeca is emotionally withdrawn and harbours considerable bitterness; she keeps her feelings, and by extension her imagination, repressed. There is no thought to her routine – just open the wardrobe door and pull out the next Chanel suit or dress (she sports a Chanel LBD layered in green for a night out). Lagerfeld does Chanel with a delight in the superfluous; he enjoys the kitsch. Rebeca buys into the label because, to her, kitsch does not exist. Chanel wearers on film appreciate irony far less than Lagerfeld himself.

More of Lagerfeld's off-the-peg designs for Chanel can be seen on Penélope Cruz in Pedro Almodóvar's Hitchcockian thriller *Broken Embraces* (*Los abrazos rotos*, 2009). Cruz plays Magdalena Rivas, a desperate woman who becomes mistress to her older boss, wealthy businessman Ernesto Martel (José Luis Gómez). Magdalena's new life gives her the money and the freedom to pursue her dreams. It also grants her admission to Chanel's exclusive couture club. Progressing from a body-scrunching grey Azzedine Alaïa suit to a swathed Chanel sheath featuring Lagerfeld's revered *trompe l'oeil* chains, she enters a new realm of fashion.

Broken Embraces is told primarily in flashback, with Magdalena's scenes taking place between 1992 and 1994. Lagerfeld gave costume designer Sonia Grande access to Chanel archives from this era, and she mixed her ensembles with selected pieces from 2007/8. The period aspect is not rammed home in the film, nor is Magdalena kitted out entirely in Chanel. Nonetheless, it becomes woefully apparent that Magdalena is trapped in an obsessive relationship, and that her allegiance to Chanel echoes this obsession. When Magdalena falls in love with another man, her sartorial bondage is fully revealed in a blue-and-red check Chanel tweed jacket, cut along classic box lines, covered in gold buttons and improbably placed non-functional zips. When Magdalena eventually finds the strength to leave Ernesto, she is dressed in a scorching red Chanel suit and matching high heels. Almodóvar's camera follows the clacking heels; they give her noise, a voice, height, but are merely an illusion. Heels are provocative because they imply dominance – but the key word here is 'imply'. For all of Magdalena's confident strutting, she is powerless. She marches past Ernesto with her head held high and he promptly pushes her down a flight of stairs.

Buttons, zips, chains – all of these purely decorative facets represent how enslaving the allure of Chanel couture can be; it is a world few can buy into, yet many covet. Money provides the freedom to choose a label that many incorrectly believe demands top-to-toe obsession. Thankfully Karl Lagerfeld has more of a sense of humour about this than Coco ever did, probably because he is not on a mission to liberate gender conventions. Coco created clothes for the modern woman; Lagerfeld created clothes for fun.

p131 top left Glamorous Victoria Abril wearing Karl
Lagerfeld for Chanel in *High Heels*

—

p131 top right This Autumn/Winter 2015 Karl Lagerfeld
ensemble combines unmistakable Chanel tweed with
Lagerfeld's oversized fit and militaristic cut

—

p131 bottom right Stéphane Audran in *Babette's Feast*,
wearing a refugee robe designed by Karl Lagerfeld for
her character

L'WREN SCOTT

DIABOLIQUE (1996)
EYES WIDE SHUT (1999)
STOKER (2012)

L'Wren Scott in 1992. Scott successfully merged celebrity styling with costume design

—

p132 Sharon Stone in dazzling red L'Wren Scott for *Diabolique*. Scott was brought on board the production at Stone's insistence

L'Wren Scott is celebrated for her reworking of the little black dress in 2006. Though her main sphere of influence in Hollywood was as a celebrity stylist to Nicole Kidman, Amy Adams, Oprah Winfrey and Ellen Barkin, among many others, Scott was officially credited as costume designer for two films, *Diabolique* starring Sharon Stone in 1996 and the thriller *Mercy* in 2000.

Scott's most recognized work as a costumier is undoubtedly *Diabolique*, a remake of creepy French classic *Les Diaboliques* (1955). Here Scott actually takes sole credit despite the film getting underway with costume designer Michael Kaplan on board. It was a troubled production for Kaplan, who had to deal with the star demands of Sharon Stone and a director not eager to rock the boat. Stone was discarding much of Kaplan's work and insisting Scott, her personal stylist, dress her instead. Eventually Kaplan left the set and never came back. Not that this had anything to do with Scott directly; Kaplan seldom had contact with the designer. To all intents and purposes, Stone's character, Nicole, an inexplicably glamorous private school teacher, was dressed entirely by Scott. This is why her wardrobe is so at odds with everyone else's in the film. Yet her look functions effectively as a stand-alone journey for Nicole, showing that Scott was more than able to interpret narrative with costume.

In *Eyes Wide Shut*, Scott kept things simple for Nicole Kidman's outwardly reserved character

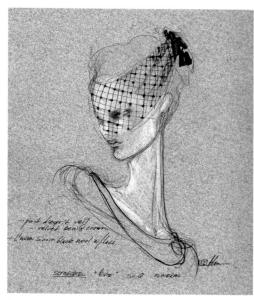

Sketch by costume designer Bart Mueller for Nicole Kidman's veil, added to a L'Wren Scott dress in *Stoker*

The feminine but powerful shapes (not a contradiction in terms) worn by Sharon Stone confirm Nicole's turn from controlling to confused and then conflicted. At the beginning of *Diabolique* Nicole wears a vivid three-tone combo of bright red, lime green and animal print. Other colours are mixed in, but one of her three signature tones is always evident: for example, a leopard-print headscarf or shoes; a bright red jacket or glossy red pants. This is in obvious contrast to her victim and lover Mia (Isabelle Adjani), also a school teacher but dressed in shapeless dresses and loose knitwear. As Nicole's plan spirals ever more out of control, her green and red tones become much darker and the leopard print disappears altogether. The loss of colour is literal in regards to Stone's pasty make up – even her ruby lips have diminished by the final scene. Scott's dressing of Sharon Stone is symbolically heavy-handed – red representing danger and green poison – but perhaps this is only because the rest of the cast are dressed so demurely by comparison?

Scott was asked by another of her celebrity clients, Nicole Kidman, to work on *Eyes Wide Shut* (1999) alongside costumier Marit Allen. This was a more harmonious affair than *Diabolique*, with Allen responsible for the bulk of the film's emblematic ensembles and props such as the Kartaruga ball masks, while Scott concentrated on Kidman's character, unfulfilled artist and wife Alice. Scott's contribution could be defined as template for the designer over the next ten years. Alice is dressed conservatively to enhance the voyeuristic sensuality of her nakedness. Her first outfit, the black gown worn at the Christmas party, covers far more that it reveals, and she continues throughout the film to wear subdued, plain clothing. Scott knew exactly what was required of her in *Eyes Wide Shut* – to compliment director Stanley Kubrick's mood, not overpower it.

L'Wren Scott's most noteworthy appearance on film before her death was in *Stoker* (2012). Again styling Nicole Kidman, she provided an off-the-rack black dress from her existing collection at the request of costumiers Kurt Swanson and Bart Mueller. Since Scott cut for tall, slim women, the dress fit Kidman like a glove. Swanson and Mueller then accessorized the dress with a veil and new collar for the funeral scene.

Scott died in March 2013 aged just 49, but with time on her side, she could have made a serious dent in cinema.

Nicole Kidman wearing a L'Wren Scott dress for the funeral
scene in *Stoker*. Costumiers Kurt and Bart added the veil

MANOLO BLAHNIK

MARIE ANTOINETTE (2006)
SEX AND THE CITY (2008)

Manolo Blahnik surrounded by shoes in his salon
—
p136 *Marie Antoinette* costumier Milena Canonero
asked Manolo Blahnik and L.C.P. di Pompei to design
all featured footwear. Canonero received the film's
only Academy Award

As shorthand for extravagance, Manolo Blahnik is familiar the world over. Blahnik was born in Spain in 1942 but, searching for a creative outlet, he moved to London in 1968 and then, at the suggestion of Diana Vreeland (who spotted some of his shoe designs and suggested that this was where his talents lay), to New York in 1970. It was here that he met designer Ossie Clark, who asked Blahnik to create shoes for his upcoming collection. Following this came prolific growth in the eighties and nineties, with recognition for Blahnik's towering heels (he hates wedges) solidified when costume designer Patricia Field chose the brand for Carrie in *Sex and the City*. His solitary credit for film, *Marie Antoinette* (2006), is significant not chiefly for his designs, but for the very fact that his name was chosen. Director Sofia Coppola was making a statement: the beautiful teen queen with a taste for opulence should have the ultimate in lavish shoes.

The footwear Blahnik created for *Marie Antoinette* consists of anachronistic eighteenth-century reproductions aimed at the female gaze. Women covet beautiful shoes, while heterosexual men covet the silhouette they produce (elongated legs; the staircase to sex), which is entirely dependent on construction (the high heel). As if by means of contrast, and to remind us that Marie Antoinette (Kirsten Dunst) was a teenage girl,

the film also features a pair of Converse trainers tossed beside the Blahniks. Shoes are the first item given to the young queen as she awakes as the wife of Louis XVI. She is naked but for a pair of pink low-heeled slippers. 'This is ridiculous', she protests. 'This is Versailles!' responds her lady-in-waiting, the Countess of Noailles (nicknamed 'Madame Etiquette' by Marie Antoinette). Even above jewellery, shoes in *Marie Antoinette* are considered the greatest of all fetishes. Adorned in saccharine colours, they are closely equated with cake – the very food that signifies Marie Antoinette's downfall. The first scene of the movie shows her lazing in wickedness, scooping a layer of pink icing as a delicate satin slipper is placed upon her foot.

    Marie Antoinette's 'I Want Candy' montage illustrates the decadence of a woman separated from reality. Shoes feature prominently, the camera drawn to their beauty as to the sparkling jewels with which the women decorate themselves. Costumier Milena Canonero wanted Manolo Blahnik to make the shoes because he was, and still is, the last word in luxury: a shoe designer who produces beautiful things relatable to our world only by desire. Blahnik used portraits of Marie Antoinette to replicate the basic shape of the era, but his creations are intentionally not period accurate. As Marie Antoinette is handed a pair of satin kitten-heel slippers, she utters, disparaging her king's mistress, 'These are so Du Barry' – too much, too flamboyant even for her.

    Marie Antoinette inspired a *Vogue* cover and spread (incidentally minus Blahnik's shoes) and countless frou-frou romantic shoots celebrating a vacuousness the fashion world is generally too embarrassed to admit. Yet the industry's most famous media outlet, *Sex and the City*, was happily obsessed with the superficial. Any designer lucky enough to be featured on the show

p138 Design sketch (left) and final shoe (right) for the *Sex and the City* movie wedding pump by Manolo Blahnik. Such is the desirability of his shoes, Blahnik has even published a coffee-table book of concept sketches
—
p139 top Kirsten Dunst wearing Manolo Blahnik shoes in *Marie Antoinette*. Look carefully and you'll spot a pair of Converse trainers in the film, too
—
p139 bottom Manolo Blahnik design sketch for *Marie Antoinette*. The deliberately gaudy colour echoes the symbol of Marie Antoinette's downfall – cake

had their profile raised immeasurably, and none more so than Manolo Blahnik, whose shoes are integral to the narrative of the first *Sex and the City* movie (2008).

    Blahnik created a pair of blue satin and brooch-encrusted high heels for the movie. When Carrie's intended, 'Mr Big', refuses a *Vogue* wedding – as Carrie herself ultimately does – she ties the knot wearing a plain vintage shop ensemble ('by no one') and blue satin Manolos; Big actually proposes a second time to Carrie using these shoes to 'seal the deal' in place of a diamond ring. Again, Blahnik's shoes surpass even jewellery. The *Sex and the City* movie was not well received by diehard fans of the show, possibly due to Carrie's rejection of her label-obsessed existence on the most important day of her life. The Blahniks remain, but as the day's one extravagance, their allure heightened by the relative modesty of Carrie's wedding attire. (Hundreds of pairs of the same design were sold by department store Neiman Marcus after the film was released.) If the most important part of Carrie is her shoes, then surely the most important shoes must be by Manolo Blahnik.

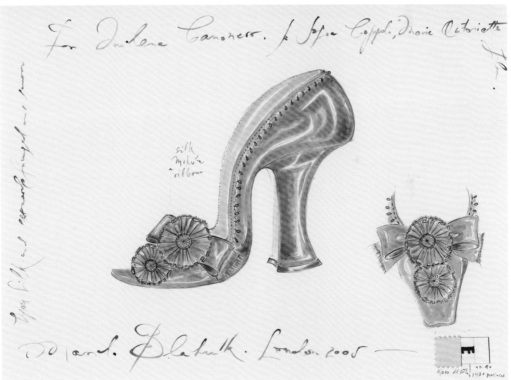

MARC JACOBS

THE DARJEELING LIMITED (2007)

Marc Jacobs at his Fall/Winter show during New York Fashion Week, February 2016. His suits were a key component of the costumes for *The Darjeeling Limited*

—

p140 Jason Schwartzman, Owen Wilson and Adrien Brody wearing Louis Vuitton by Marc Jacobs suits in *The Darjeeling Limited*

'I didn't save mine', Peter Whitman (Adrien Brody) announces as he holds a lifeless child in his arms. This is the most important line in *The Darjeeling Limited* (2007): it encapsulates the three principal characters' preoccupation with possessions. The Whitman brothers argue over their deceased father's possessions; they seek possessions they don't need, such as clogs, pepper spray, and a poisonous snake; and, as with insecure ladies' man Jack (Jason Schwartzman), they treat people as possessions. They are not bad men, just Western men. So what better way to embody this rationale than an 11-piece Louis Vuitton luggage set to cart unceremoniously around India, with each brother wearing a near-identical Louis Vuitton by Marc Jacobs suit? There's irony here, since Marc Jacobs has always been keen to steer away from being associated with any trend or revolution. Many consider that the early nineties grunge movement or oversize buttons or checked flannel shirts somehow 'belong' to the designer. However, the 'Jacobs' look is one of constant reinvention.

Jacobs is a fashion prodigy. He pursued the calling at an early age, graduating from the prestigious Parsons School of Design at 21, and then went on to produce his first collection for Reuben Thomas's Sketchbook label, inspired by the costumes in the films *Purple Rain* and *Amadeus*. This was the start of his

fashion journey and his first meaningful excursion into the use of colour to convey narrative. What's more, like Coco Chanel before him (see page 48), Jacobs directly referenced clothes from the street. He did not invent grunge, but he reinterpreted it on the catwalk, where, propagating a customary fashion paradox, it was reinterpreted in turn for the (high) street. A sharp businessman, Jacobs set up his own international brand to capitalize on early recognition. He was artistic director at Louis Vuitton until 2014.

      Through lack of availability more than anything else, Jacobs has officially been involved in the costumes of only one feature so far: friend and director Wes Anderson's atmospheric travelogue *The Darjeeling Limited*. Overall costumier for the film was Milena Canonero, a VIP with a CV that includes *A Clockwork Orange*, *The Shining* and *Chariots of Fire* – evidently not someone to feel intimidated by collaborating with a famous fashion designer. It was Anderson's idea to bring Jacobs in, but his involvement was limited to a custom luggage set and the leads' suits. Anderson has admitted on several occasions that he chooses to give his characters uniforms. All of his most popular creations – Margot in *The Royal Tenenbaums* (see pages 72, 102), Gustave in *The Grand Budapest Hotel*, Max in *Rushmore* – exhibit a uniform, whether official attire

p142 Mark Jacobs's designs for *The Darjeeling Limited* are a modern update of the classic American grey flannel suit

—

p143 left Marc Jacobs's acting debut in *Disconnect*. He has yet to appear on screen again

—

p143 right Marc Jacobs Spring 2015 collection at Mercedes-Benz Fashion Week. Jacobs retains a uniform, military look for both men and women, and the oversize buttons hark back to an early signature look

or merely visual characterization. Their clothes define them as, in Western society, regardless of intention, clothes define all of us.

The *Darjeeling Limited* suits, a variation on the classic American grey flannel, were tailored in-house at Louis Vuitton. They are the glue holding these fragile brothers together as something approaching a family unit. Their form conjures up that typical Wes Anderson vibe of a timeless parallel world, but, as always, some-how inexplicably leaning towards the late sixties. Each two-button single-breasted suit features slim notch lapels, wide-spaced three-button surgeon's cuffs (in other words, functional rather than decorative buttons), a rear half-belt, and low-rise trousers. Jacobs kept a rein on anything too fanciful. His suits are unusual enough to be contemporary, yet traditional enough to feel classic. The lightly padded late-fifties jacket shoulder recalls another American out of his depth in an alien environment, Cary Grant in *North by Northwest* (1959), while the Norfolk half-belt, a throwback to what is in essence a twenties tracksuit, signifies that the Whitman brothers are more prepared to globetrot than they ever realized. Jacobs's input in *The Darjeeling Limited* is front and centre, though thankfully not flagged as a go-to citation for trainee hipsters. The LV luggage, with its forties-esque *Little Prince* illustrations,

as created by Anderson's brother Eric (who also designed Owen Wilson's $3,000 'solar system' loafers), also becomes an essential component of the plot.

Marc Jacobs later tried his hand at acting in an impressive ensemble piece called *Disconnect* (2011), but before the film was released he theatrically retired from the profession without warning. Jacobs clearly enjoys the lure of the movies, even if he cannot commit to the role of even part-time actor. However, if he achieves little more on screen than *The Darjeeling Limited*, his legacy as an artist who understands the craft of costuming distinct to that of fashion will remain justifiably intact.

MARY QUANT

THE HAUNTING (1963)
THE WILD AFFAIR (1963)
GEORGY GIRL (1966)
TWO FOR THE ROAD (1967)

Mary Quant sketching in a zip-neck mini-dress – similar in design to the green and white dress she provided for *Two for the Road*

—

p144 Audrey Hepburn wearing a Mary Quant mini-dress in *Two for the Road*, a radical departure from her habitual Givenchy attire on screen

Mary Quant didn't spend long designing for cinema. She herself admits that it was cripplingly difficult, with rigorous shooting schedules impeding her already demanding life as a fashion designer. Quant's tenure on film lasted just four years, spanning *The Haunting* (1963) to *Two for the Road* (1967).

British-made but American-financed, *The Haunting* came during a period when, although established in the UK, Quant had yet to break in the USA. At this point she was not associated with inventing the miniskirt – a credit she now shares with designers André Courrèges and John Bates – but for cutting and dying unusual fabrics such as PVC and oilskin to make coats and dresses. *The Haunting* required Quant to inject a clean, modern quality into the character of Theodora (Claire Bloom). Theodora's look became a variation on the mod subculture with which Quant was linked, though toned down for more conservative American audiences. Another aspect to be underplayed was Theodora's sexuality. Quant dressed her as a beatnik in a black roll-neck, cigarette pants and heeled boots, while deliberately heightening her femininity via a giraffe-skin coat with Mongolian lambswool collar. Reflecting the character's inoffensive, if flirtatious, interactions with fitful Eleanor (Julie Harris), Quant pulled away from the butch lesbian cliché towards a more progressive feminine aesthetic.

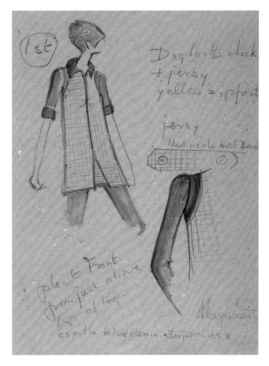

Quant's next film outing was *The Wild Affair* (1963), in the same year as *The Haunting*. Marjorie (Nancy Kwan) is a soon-to-be-married secretary hoping for one great office fling before giving up her job and starting a family. This is a classic mid-sixties farce, dripping in misogyny. Quant provided all the clothes for Kwan's character who, at the time, was seen as a forward-thinking girl. Kwan's parade of outfits culminates in an above-the-knee sleeveless shift for the big office party. Funnily enough, the dress is actually purchased for her by a man she intends to sleep with. Mary Quant's clothes were made for go-getters, or in the case of *The Wild Affair,* as gifts or 'inducements'. They were far from cheap. A Quant girl had means.

Quant's most memorable costume outing was *Georgy Girl* (1966), featuring what would come to be defined as her signature look – unembellished lines, sparse by the standards of the previous decade's heavily accessorized silhouette. Tempted back to the screen by the lure of dressing model Charlotte Rampling in her first credited performance, Quant went all out: jabot collar, Peter Pan collar mini-dress, Mondrian shift, fur coat. Although the film was shot in black and white, Quant's clothes stand out a mile. Meredith (Rampling) is the opposite of lovable kooky lead character Georgy (Lynn Redgrave). While Georgy flops around in oversized jumpers, Meredith zips across London wearing

p146 left Although not explicitly referenced in the script, Claire Bloom's character in *The Haunting* is a lesbian. Quant rejected the then-typical 'butch' aesthetic for soft fur and animal print

—

p146 top right Biracial actress Nancy Kwan in *The Wild Affair* is in every way the 'Mary Quant girl': youthful, energetic, petite

—

p146 bottom right Sketch for a classic Mary Quant mini-dress

—

p147 left Sneering Charlotte Rampling in *Georgy Girl*. Mary Quant provided all her clothes for the film, though her character – a moneyed, bitchy socialite – is hardly aspirational

—

p147 right Charlotte Rampling in *Georgy Girl* wearing a Mary Quant fur coat and (wedding) dress, the hem of which is, as always, above the knee

one immaculate ensemble after another. Quant's costumes in this context are used to paint Meredith as a selfish, attention-seeking vamp, used by director Silvio Narizzano to make a statement about stagnating culture. Meredith may look wonderful but she is hollow inside, unlike Georgy who is caring, empathetic and content to be seen as a frump; designer fashion here enhances the film's own narrative.

Mary's Quant final film is her best known simply because of its lead actress. In *Two for the Road* (1967) Audrey Hepburn abandoned her go-to Givenchy for off-the-rack by designers of the moment, such as Paco Rabanne, V de V and Mary Quant (see pages 108, 155). The rocky marriage of her character, Joanna, can be mapped out by her increasingly on-trend garments. She begins a fresh-faced girl in jeans, Shetland sweater and leather belt, and ends a tired, embittered, though undeniably stylish woman in green-and-white trim mini-dress with Oliver Goldsmith 'bug eye' sunglasses. Quant supplied only two garments for the movie – the green-and-white mini and a red-and-yellow-striped jersey shift based on her own T-shirt dress, with added white shirt collar and cuffs.

After the worldwide success of *Two for the Road,* Mary Quant no longer needed film to publicize her work. She never designed for cinema again, instead concentrating entirely on the world of fashion.

NINO CERRUTI

PRETTY WOMAN (1990)
INDECENT PROPOSAL (1993)
IN THE LINE OF FIRE (1993)

Cerruti sketch for one of Redford's suits in *Indecent Proposal*. The double-breasted silhouette is a classic 6-on-2 (six buttons, two that fasten) design

p148 Robert Redford wearing Nino Cerruti in *Indecent Proposal*. Redford's shirts sport single fastening buttons (not cufflinks) to reflect his character's blue-collar roots

Chances are, if you have seen a movie, you have seen a Cerruti suit. They really are that ubiquitous. Via head stylist and owner Nino, grandson of the original founders, Cerruti has become part of the fabric of cinema. From initial appearances in the sixties and seventies, to its heyday during the eighties and nineties, the gentleman's Cerruti lounge suit has been worn by just about every legendary Hollywood actor in the business. Cerruti probably has more 'with thanks to' credits than the State of New York.

When Nino took over the family business in the fifties he began to clothe the main Parisian draws of the day. Jean-Paul Belmondo asked Cerruti to provide Victorian period costumes for him in *Up to His Ears* (*Les tribulations d'un Chinois en Chine*, 1965). Then came thirties-style gangster suits for Alain Delon in *Borsalino* (1970), which also featured Belmondo, and the process blossomed from there. Cerruti did not launch an official menswear collection until 1967, which was when it also established its diffusion line, '1881'. Costumiers like Cerruti because the brand's look is not overly distinct, and thus dateable. Plus, with its background as a textile manufacturer, Cerruti can tailor from fine fabrics quickly and in volume. It is perfectly poised as an outfitter to the movie industry.

So what exactly is the Cerruti look? In terms of the gentleman's suit (for which the brand remains most famous, despite a flourishing women's line), this has changed comparatively little since the fifties. Yet when Nino Cerruti launched the 'Hitman' collection for men in 1957 it was seen as radical. Nino kept the V-shaped body that had been popular for over 20 years, a style that involved elongating the jacket torso by widening the shoulders and nipping the waist, then he removed much of the extraneous internal padding, softening the suit's overall silhouette. The cut was full and has remained so ever since, just without the rigid structure; drape became key. The most typical Cerruti look – defining the brand – is on Richard Gere in *Pretty Woman* (1990). Gere plays Edward Lewis, a hotshot West Coast international businessman. His most memorable attire is a mid-grey, 4-on-1 double-breasted suit with peaked lapels. This has never been the most fashionable form of suit, certainly after the forties, yet because of its imposing profile it still holds sway in the corporate world. The ensemble Cerruti made for Gere was so well liked that it sparked a mini-revival in the double-breasted suit – a style the designer had previously promoted heavily on catwalks in 1983. This revival was short lived, however, and present-day double-breasted suits are only popular when cut far higher and tighter across the chest.

Richard Gere provides another connection to Cerruti because of his long-time association with Giorgio Armani. Gere made Armani's name in *American*

Gigolo and to this day remains a loyal customer. Of course Gere also wears Cerruti, on screen and off, and Armani's first break came as a young designer at the house. Armani joined Cerruti in 1961, tasked with the 'Hitman' range, and he continued to work there for the rest of the decade. Cerruti, along with French designer Daniel Hechter, was a major inspiration for Armani's soft tailored look in *American Gigolo* (see page 80).

Despite some controversial claims in his career, such as designing the white suit Sharon Stone wore in *Basic Instinct* (that was costumier Ellen Mirojnick) or creating the look for TV series *Miami Vice* (Jodi Tillen), Nino Cerruti does seem to appreciate the role of costume better than most fashion designers. Nino wanted the Cerruti attire provided for Robert Redford in *Indecent Proposal* (1993) to be as sumptuous and elegant as possible – after all, he was playing someone who offers $1 million dollars for a night with another man's wife. Yet Redford's John Gage was self-made, so Cerruti was persuaded that the fancy double cuffs and cufflinks he was pushing would not have worked for the character. With fashion designers, priority number one is always to make the client look as good as possible, but for costume designers clothes must be, first and foremost, apt for the character.

This concept of dressing for character only, no matter how high profile the star, is also apparent in the suits Cerruti provided for Clint Eastwood as Secret Service agent Frank Horrigan in the 1993 film *In the*

p150 The Cerruti 4-on-1 (four buttons, one that fastens) double-breasted suit worn by Richard Gere in *Pretty Woman* is a concession to the fashion of the time, but also gives his character a more laidback air

—

p151 left Note the low button stance of Robert Redford's white suit in *Indecent Proposal;* it elongates the body, so the wearer needs long legs to match

—

p151 right Secret Serviceman Clint Eastwood's grey/blue-tinged suits for *In the Line of Fire* were made by Cerruti. They are all single-breasted to accommodate drawing a handgun

Line of Fire. Cerruti hoped to outfit Eastwood in the trendier double-breasted line he was promoting at the time. However, because Horrigan is armed, his suits had to be single-breasted to allow the speedy drawing of a handgun. One could argue that Horrigan would be unlikely to purchase Cerruti suits anyway; his character seems more of a J.C. Penney guy. Yet even rugged Clint Eastwood wanted to appear as debonair as possible on screen. Thus fashion and film have to coexist because, since the dawn of cinema, movie stars have always liked to appear their best.

PACO RABANNE

TWO FOR THE ROAD (1967)
BARBARELLA (1968)

Paco Rabanne (metal)working in 1968. The couturier used anything but typical fabrics

—

p152 Rabanne was part of a team that created Jane Fonda's costumes for *Barbarella*. His aesthetic is clearly visible in this PVC one-piece with thigh-high boots

Spanish-born designer Paco Rabanne is an innovator to the highest degree, his garments tending more towards mobile art installations than clothes people can wear. His debut show, '12 Unwearable Dresses', in 1966 was a look into the future, a calling card for a man who thought nothing of bending pieces of metal around his models on a workbench and calling it a dress.

Director Stanley Donan wanted a very different look for Audrey Hepburn in his comedy drama *Two for the Road* (1967; see also pages 17, 144). The film, a story of a young couple's difficult marriage, was a departure for Hepburn because she was, in essence, playing a real person. In movies such as Donan's own *Charade* (1963) and *How to Steal a Million* (1966; see pages 111, 112), she exists more as an aspirational poster image. In *Two For the Road*, Hepburn plays Joanna, one half of a bumpy partnership with husband Mark (Albert Finney). Donan was well aware of his leading lady's connection to couturier Hubert de Givenchy, and in fact was good friends with the designer, but for this picture Hepburn needed to be shopped for; she had to wear clothes that any woman, albeit a well-heeled one, could purchase off the rack. Casting Givenchy aside was difficult for Hepburn, although wardrobe supervisor Clare Rendlesham ensured she never appeared in anything less than

Rabanne continues to experiment with unconventional materials, including this sculptural design from his Autumn/Winter 1999 collection

This shimmery Rosemary Rodriquez for Paco Rabanne 2002 Spring/Summer piece refines the chainmail effect of Audrey Hepburn's *Two for the Road* disc dress

spectacular. *Two for the Road* is Hepburn's foremost fashion movie, but for once clothes were not specially designed or altered for the actress. Any woman with enough change in her purse could look like Joanna.

Rendlesham selected two items from Paco Rabanne for Hepburn, a yellow plastic visor and the final-act showstopper, a silver cocktail slip constructed of chainmail and mottled metal discs. The visor is only glimpsed, worn with a red-and-yellow-striped Mary Quant dress for mere seconds of screen time. However the Rabanne silver disc dress is integral to the final act. The garment was so awkward and uncomfortable it was near impossible for Hepburn to move properly or even sit down, thus reflecting her relationship with Mark at this point: prickly, difficult, and in danger of being abandoned entirely. Rabanne's disc dress is probably his most iconic creation, not specifically due to being featured in *Two for the Road*, but because it symbolizes the designer's desire to use anything other than conventional materials in his creations.

Paco Rabanne is best remembered for creating costumes for Jane Fonda in certifiable science-fiction camp-fest *Barbarella* (1968). In actual fact, Rabanne was part of a team comprising costumier Jacques Fonteray, Pietro Farani, *Barbarella* comic-book artist Jean-Claude Forest and director Roger Vadim, and Rabanne's role was limited to inspiration for Fonda's last-act ensemble of green sleeveless leotard with acetate plastic fringing. Nonetheless, his aesthetic is all over *Barbarella*, from a breakaway polyvinyl spacesuit gradually revealing Fonda's nakedness, to a triple-belt-buckle silver PVC one-piece with attached thigh-high boots. His desire to stretch the definition of what could rightly be termed 'clothing' is imperative for a movie in which the central character's attire is torn, bitten, stripped or otherwise removed from her body.

Barbarella has acquired a feminist reading over recent years, though this is mainly due to Fonda's own active political stance. Certainly a film about a woman spreading a message of copulation throughout the galaxy is very much sixties gender liberation.

This striking but uncomfortable Paco Rabanne disc
dress was Audrey Hepburn's most loathed costume
for *Two for the Road*

The armour-like effect of Rabanne's tiling technique
is especially evident in Jane Fonda's green sleeveless
leotard for *Barbarella*

Barbarella was shot on a soundstage in Italy, which
is also where Fonda's costumes were made by Pietro
Farani's tailoring house. Rabanne's green leotard
covered with plastic tiles is one of the most impressive
garments in the film. Fonda's 'secret uniform of the
revolution', featuring a singular breastplate with a clear
piece that exposes one of Fonda's own breasts, was
not created by the designer but is typical of his designs.
Drawing attention to erogenous zones, if not actually
revealing them, is a hallmark of Rabanne's work.
His outfits are often built on the body. Ironic then
that even though his clothes fit like armour they offer
scant real-world protection. You would not want to go
into battle wearing a chainmail dress, no matter how
fabulous it looked.

For a movie where plot is hardly the driving
force, *Barbarella* works hard to legitimize its protago-
nist's many (eight) costume changes. Admittedly these
largely come about post-coitus, but at least they are
not imagined out of thin air. 'Could you pass me a garment?' asks Barbarella two minutes after overloading
the Excessive (orgasm 'torture') Machine. Thankfully
Rabanne's ornately constructed leotard with Cavalier-
style boots are lying on the floor nearby.

Paco Rabanne's legacy in cinema will always
be *Barbarella*, but it should be *Two for the Road*. Its
chainmail disc dress and plastic visor completely
belong to the designer, and they sum up his whole
approach to fashion impeccably. You do not wear
Rabanne; you display it.

PIERRE BALMAIN

AND GOD CREATED WOMAN (1956)
THE RELUCTANT DEBUTANTE (1958)
THE MILLIONAIRESS (1960)

Pierre Balmain with a two of his models at London
Airport, 1950. The fifties, with its chic lines and shapely
silhouette, was Balmain's most prolific period
—
p156 Sophia Loren in a Pierre Balmain satin corset
for *The Millionairess*. The alleged cost of all of Loren's
costumes in the film was £75,000 (unadjusted)

After World War II there was a surge of glamour in the fashion industry. Certain austerity rules still applied but, in Paris at least, designers wanted a return to sculptured form. Judging by the success of precision-constructed collections by the likes of Jacques Fath, Christian Dior and Pierre Balmain, women wanted this too. Balmain was a businessman who created couture to wear. Floral-esque nipped-waist dresses with billowing skirts may not have been the most comfortable garments, but they were functional, otherwise they would never have made it onto his racks.

Although Dior is credited with inventing the 'New Look' with his 1947 line that, after years of shapelessness, re-emphasized the bust and hips, Balmain contested that his own label, launched in 1945, was in on the act first. He had in fact worked alongside Dior at Lucien Lelong, but Balmain was not about to concede anything quietly, doing whatever it took to promote his house among the Hollywood elite. He designed costumes for dozens of films in his career and provided gowns for many others, dressing such industry talent as Marlene Dietrich, Sophia Loren, Brigitte Bardot and, most interestingly, the willowy and very un-Hollywood-like figure of Kay Kendall.

And God Created Woman (*Et Dieu... créa la femme*, 1956) cemented Balmain's name, and Brigitte Bardot's even more so. He provided key costumes for her career-defining turn as misunderstood provocateur Juliette. Director Roger Vadim lapped up Bardot's figure like a grubby voyeur in the bushes. However, most of Juliette's sensuality is implied. Apart from the scenes when she is naked or semi-naked, Balmain's clothes emphasize Juliette's form by covering it. The film was a showcase for his practical, purposeful designs that, while formal in today's terms, could almost be seen as casual in mid-fifties small-town France. Many of Juliette's ensembles follow a shirt dress pattern featuring closed or open semi-spread collars – even her wedding dress, with rows of buttons that are sometimes functioning, sometimes decorative. In context these buttons imply Juliette's repression. She may appear sexually active to those around her, but this is their (and our) construct not hers – she just plays along with it. The one time Juliette snubs attention (clothed in a full-length belted coat), a bus she is waiting for drives straight past, ignoring her.

The erotic symbolism of fastened and unfastened buttons is established with Juliette's first dress: long, shirt style, belted, buttoned far from indecently at the neck but open beyond her knees at the hem. When marooned on a beach, Juliette teases our gaze even further with all buttons unfastened on a different shirt dress, this time soaking wet, with only a belt retaining her modesty. This is the moment Juliette finally succumbs to type and cheats on her husband. No longer repressed or merely deviant, she has become poisonous. Her fine-striped green wrap-over skirt and the line of fabric-covered buttons she tears open to dance for ogling men represent a fall from grace. Juliette is led to believe that she has nothing to offer without her sexualized form. Bardot also wears denim jeans in the film, her character set apart from other more decoratively dressed women as being vaguely masculine. She is open, liberated and, more often than not, barefoot – another facet that encourages narrow-minded perception of her apparent sexual recklessness.

The Reluctant Debutante (1958), starring Kay Kendall, was a Hollywood production. Even though Balmain was primarily known for his work in French cinema, he dressed Kendall for her role as aristocratic

p158 **left and right** The costumes created by Balmain for *And God Created Woman* are not provocative or risqué; conversely they reveal Brigitte Bardot's desirable figure by hiding it

—

p159 Balmain's costumes for Bardot in *And God Created Woman* draw attention to Bardot's form without violating censorship codes

We chose this in Paris

... for its debonair dash ... for the new shoulder-line, dropped from the curve of the horseshoe collar. Bold-checked nine-tenths coat, buttoned with discs of ocean pearl, feature of the Collections. Pictured among treasures in the fabulous apartment of Helena Rubinstein on the Quai de Bethune.

Available from Model Coats towards the end of March.

Photographed specially for Debenhams by Peter Clark

Pierre Balmain at Debenhams

Debenham & Freebody Wigmore Street London W1 Langham 4444

p160 top Kay Kendall (left) was recovering from a pelvic fracture when Pierre Balmain costumed her for *The Reluctant Debutante*. She was fitted for most of her gowns lying down to ease the pain

—

p160 bottom A 1959 advertisement for 'Pierre Balmain at Debenhams', as high fashion moves into the increasingly important high-street market

—

p161 left Sophia Loren in *The Millionairess* in a flower-pot hat and swathed in fur. Her character's attempts to 'dress down' are hardly any less subtle than this

—

p161 right Sophia Loren in a Balmain wiggle dress in *The Millionairess*, still managing to look exceptional even after leaping into the River Thames

English stepmother Sheila Broadbent, alongside Helen Rose, who created costumes for the rest of the movie. Balmain's clothes are bold and distinctively feminine in a metropolitan fifties style. He saw Kendall's as a catwalk body rather than the era's typically voluptuous pin-up. Balmain's ensembles enveloped Kendall, lengthening rather than concealing her frame. A red silk evening sheath topped with faux fur wrap implies both Sheila's class status and the actress's own sense of humour. *The Reluctant Debutante* continued Balmain's on- and off-screen sartorial relationship with Kendall. His biggest challenge for film, however, would require an altogether different approach, dressing the impossibly curvaceous form of Sophia Loren.

London-set romantic comedy *The Millionairess* (1960) is fully justified in its extravagant attire. Sophia Loren plays Epifania, spoilt inheritor of a small fortune from her deceased father. *The Millionairess* needs Loren, about the only woman in the world striking enough not to be overshadowed by the jaw-dropping creations. Yet for all his grandiose designs, Balmain understands that these are costumes not fashion. Loren's character must not, and never does, appear any less than believably dressed for her world. If narrative

allows, Loren wears a fresh ensemble for each scene. She even gets changed into a purple wiggle dress (symbolic colour of death) with matching wide-brimmed hat and bow, to make a half-hearted attempt at suicide by jumping in the river Thames. Further into the film, Balmain costumes Epifania in born-again white as she opens a clinic 'for the poor'. In her slashed-neck sheath with matching swing coat trimmed in mink, low-heel white shoes and white flowerpot hat she is a rich do-gooder desperate to appear interesting. Hilariously, Epifania attempts to prove her business skills by going 'incognito' in a spaghetti factory wearing about the finest-grain grey leather dress, matching bag and fedora money can buy. Balmain re-employs his staples from the mid- to late fifties, such as fur coats, fur shrugs, belted wiggle dresses and knee-length sheaths, and Loren's severely boned corset bends her to the designer's requisite hourglass silhouette.

Sixties London was moving away from sculptured form towards skimming a boyish, less explicitly gendered figure, epitomized by young model Twiggy. *The Millionairess* was cinema's last great hurrah for thirty-something elitist couture. The future now belonged to the young – and the high street.

PIERRE CARDIN

BEAUTY AND THE BEAST (1946)
THE GAME IS OVER (1966)
A DANDY IN ASPIC (1968)

Pierre Cardin in his workshop in 1975
—
p162 Jane Fonda as Renée wearing trademark Pierre
Cardin fur in French/Italian production *The Game Is Over*

For a designer who cut his teeth at Christian Dior during the launch of its abstractly feminine 'New Look' in 1947, Pierre Cardin's trademark style of bold geometric shapes that ignore the female form rather than shape it may seem a world away. However, like Dior, Cardin is fascinated by architecture and structure; he just builds on the body in a different way. Cardin is the most merchandised designer on the planet. His name adorns everything from toiletries to automobile interiors. Cinema was just another way for Cardin's work to reach the masses, although his start as a costumier really came about by accident. At his zenith during the sixties, he only designed sporadically in the seventies before disappearing from movies in pursuit of other projects. What portfolio we do have, incorporating voluptuous gowns for Elizabeth Taylor in *The V.I.P.s* (1963) and clean chic on Jane Fonda in *The Game Is Over* (*La curée*, 1966), summarizes everything the Cardin name stands for.

Cardin was briefly a cutter for legendary experimentalist Elsa Schiaparelli before sewing for Paquin in 1945. On joining the house, Cardin met director Jean Cocteau along with fashion illustrator Christian Bérard and actress Jean Marais, and was asked to assist with creating costumes for Cocteau's adaptation of *Beauty and the Beast* (*La belle et la bête*, 1946); the film has an

extravagant, historically overstated look, swathed in fabric, similar to Paquin's own aesthetic. Cardin moved on to designing at Dior before founding his own house in 1950. He showed his first collection in 1953, and his main impact on screen occurred just over a decade later.

Cardin dressed Jane Fonda for *The Game Is Over* as a rich plaything, alienated and alienating through her choice of clothing. Even though her character, Renée, sports lavish fur as part of almost all her outfits, either a hat, coat or embellishing a frock, she attempts to deny her rich lifestyle with an inappropriateness of attire. Her trapeze dress in lemon chiffon, its hem trimmed in ostrich feathers, is a light-hearted protest during a party at her husband's home. Renée falls in love and begins an affair with her stepson, which further intensifies her rejection of elitist couture. Cardin makes certain Renée's look remains sincere yet accessible, as she is eventually to become our point of empathy. She alternates high-waisted slim pants and simple headscarves with a sumptuous white silk sheath and matching ostrich-trimmed cloak, or a below-the-knee taupe shift with unique serrated hem that gives the semblance of a paper doll. Although she plays dress-up, Renée is most comfortable in rudimentary gym attire of legwarmers, plain white tee and pink cotton kickers. Renée's garments deliberately counter her environment. In one moment she leaps from a brand new red Mustang into a battered Land Rover wearing a spotless fur-topped dogtooth woollen coat. Later she allows herself to be driven fully clothed into a lake. Finally, Renée attempts to drown herself wearing a brown fox fur coat, fishnet tights and slouch leather boots. She loves what she wears, just for the sheer fashion, yet despises its isolating exclusivity.

Spy thriller *A Dandy in Aspic* (1968) is a frothier showcase of Cardin's talents. He was hired to create costumes for star Laurence Harvey and newcomer Mia Farrow. Fashion as costume was becoming trendy; just weeks before shooting commenced, Harvey and Farrow were invited to Cardin's boutique for a showing of his latest collection. The event was filmed by an excited media, and Farrow even tried on dresses for the cameras. Stopping short of an actual tie-in, Cardin promoted a dandy aesthetic through his outlets when the film was released. Customers could buy the look of the movie, if not specific ensembles.

Perhaps the most noteworthy thing about *A Dandy in Aspic* is that the dandy in question, Harvey's Russian double-agent Eberlin, is hardly flamboyant. His brown corduroy Norfolk-style suit is worn with pink shirt, cocktail cuffs and a black tie. The suit is accented with leather: leather lapels, buttons, trim, even leather elbow patches. Further into the story, Eberlin sports a single-breasted grey chalkstriped suit with narrow vents. The

vents in particular, their slight, scarcely functional cut, are indicative of Cardin's unfussy methodology.

Mia Farrow as Swinging Sixties photographer Caroline does not have a multitude of changes but rather a handful of memorable outfits. Exhibiting Cardin's finery, however, was evidently not director Anthony Mann's primary concern (unfortunately he died before shooting completed, leaving Harvey to finish). The sky-blue shift covered in jewels and beads from her first scene is painstakingly decorated yet hardly registers; another spectacular Cardin creation, a short black trapeze dress with red collar, red trim and huge red triangle across the midriff, is hidden under a black mini trench coat most of the time. But even in only scant glimpses, Cardin's love of geometric shapes and immaculate lines is clear. His look shines through yet functions within the narrative. The rectilinear and curvilinear lines, stripes, circles and crosses all contribute to the pressure trapping and constricting Eberlin inside his deceitful world.

After the few films he contributed to in the sixties, Cardin's cinematic input became more of an influence than anything else. He did design some of Patrick Macnee's costumes for *The Avengers* television series, and certainly informed Alun Hughes's trendsetting mod attire for Diana Rigg, if not created it personally. Cardin is more vibe than name; he is the sixties in a suit.

PRADA

QUANTUM OF SOLACE (2008)
THE GREAT GATSBY (2013)
THE GRAND BUDAPEST HOTEL (2014)

Prada's sketch for Daisy Buchanan's chandelier dress
in *The Great Gatsby*

—

p166 This cocktail ensemble for Carey Mulligan as Daisy
Buchanan in *The Great Gatsby*, designed and made by
Miuccia Prada, was comprised of steel rings and crystal
droplets, and dubbed the 'chandelier dress' by Mulligan

Established in Italy over a hundred years ago, Prada is lucky to still be around at all. If it were not for founder Mario Prada's granddaughter, Miuccia, taking the reins from her mother in 1970 and expanding globally, the company would probably not have made it out of the decade. Consequently Prada thrived, even behind a mountain of debt, as a brand influenced by nostalgic glamour but with a delicate modernistic touch.

Apart from Prada's appearances in cinema, either as a costume collaboration or shopped off-the-peg, they have a keen interest in film-making as a twenty-first-century marketing tool. Prada have produced several fashion mini-movies with directors such as Roman Polanski and Wes Anderson, some of which do not even feature their clothing. In early 2014 they teamed up with costumiers Michael Wilkinson (with Tim Martin), Arianne Phillips and Milena Canonero to construct a series of installations. This 'Iconoclasts' revival from 2009 is the first time a brand has reached out to costume designers to join forces and not the other way around.

Prada are not necessarily easy to spot on film. Their black crepe sweetheart-neckline dress with rose detail and ruche bow provided for Olga Kurylenko as Camille Montes in *Quantum of Solace* (2008) is beautifully finished but fundamentally nondescript.

This particular little black dress is worn for the scenes in which special agent Montes and James Bond are pursued across the Bolivian desert. Costume designer Louise Frogley wanted to use a trouser suit as it would fit the action more comfortably, but felt a dress made more sense for the climate. The Prada LBD takes what might traditionally be perceived as action attire (e.g., jeans, bodysuit, pants) and spins the notion on its head; any garment can be action attire, providing it doesn't have to survive unscathed. Miuccia Prada made 20 identical black dresses in one week for *Quantum of Solace*, most of which were destroyed during filming. Prada also provided a party gown for Gemma Arterton as MI6 operative Strawberry Fields.

The costumes for *The Great Gatsby* (2013) – featuring Brooks Brothers menswear (see page 32) and Tiffany and Co. jewellery, but mainly Prada – created a wave of hysteria. Prada was reputedly providing the whole wardrobe for Carey Mulligan as drippy heroine Daisy Buchanan. *Vogue* magazine had the exclusive, proving that costume and fashion can mix, providing the fashion is couture enough to kick-start an entire trend. The trend in question would be twenties flapper, and yet it never really took off. *The Great Gatsby* eventually opened in spring 2013, after being held back

from Christmas; when the film finally appeared, the fashion audience, despite months of being drip-fed hype about the clothes, was ready to move on. The pseudo-flapper girl spread appearing in the press several months prior to release were already two seasons out of date.

Moreover, this turned out to be another tale of inflated brand involvement, as if fashion media had learned nothing from the *Black Swan*/Rodarte affair three years earlier (see page 178). The *Great Gatsby* collaboration between Catherine Martin and Prada, however, was publically amicable. The partnership was put together by the film's director Baz Luhrmann because of his twenty-year friendship with Miuccia. Martin, Lurhmann's costumier and wife, embraced the collaboration, such as it was, although the press wanted it to be so much more. Miuccia provided only 40 gowns for the film, used exclusively on extras during the two big party scenes, and one dress, the 'chandelier' worn by Carey Mulligan. Prada certainly did not costume Mulligan for the entire movie. The dresses were adapted from Prada's archive and its secondary line 'Miu Miu', 2010 Spring/Summer and Autumn/Winter collections, which were apparently far more twenties-influenced than Muiccia realized. The chandelier

dress is a revision of catwalk 'look 33' from Prada's 2010 Spring/Summer line. Made from a web of shimmering crystal drops topped with a two-tier fur stole, it is Prada all over – elegantly refined with a nod to the past. That it was heavy and uncomfortable for Mulligan to wear is not an issue so much as its uniqueness; this was not a look any woman could easily replicate, so it was largely abandoned by the press as an unobtainable object of beauty. Prada's contribution to *The Great Gatsby*, then, was mainly the glistening flapper dresses worn by party-going extras, which are hardly seen in the finished movie. The Prada/*Gatsby* partnership added up to far more on paper than it did on screen.

More recently, Prada provided a World War II-era leather Kradmantel (motorcycle dispatch rider's coat) worn by Willem Dafoe as Jopling in *The Grand Budapest Hotel* (2014). Costumier Milena Canonero and her tailor created the toile (early fabric mock-up of a garment), which was then manufactured by Prada and lined in red wool on its return. This association brings little to the movie itself, but allows Prada to keep their hand in the medium. The brand genuinely seem far more interested in what they can provide for cinema than take away, which is probably why their filmic collaborations continue to be so harmonious.

RAF SIMONS
FOR JIL SANDER

I AM LOVE (2009)

Raf Simons at the Council of Fashion Designers of
America Awards in 2014. Simons won the International
Award for his work at Dior after moving on from Jil Sander

—

p170 Tilda Swinton's costume as Emma Recchi in *I Am
Love*. Raf Simons provided all the actress's ensembles
under instruction from costumier Antonella Cannarozzi

Born in Belgium in 1968, Raf Simons is a pioneer
in the fashion world. He established his own
self-titled label during the mid-nineties and it
still flourishes today. Simons is going from strength to
strength. Already in his career Simons has been a furni-
ture designer and chief creative director of two prominent houses (not including his own). He launched his
first men's collection in 1995. This remained his focus
until he was chosen to head Jil Sander in 2005, producing both mens- and womenswear. Jil Sander, which is
owned by Prada, was not at this point a brand known
for bold creativity, but rather clean lines and stark minimalism. Simons's response was to provisionally swap
the house dressmakers and tailors around and update
the line by gently modernizing its silhouette while
experimenting with new cutting ideas and fabrics. His
collections for Jil Sander were a tremendous success
and opened the door for his role as head of Christian
Dior in 2012, following disgraced John Galliano's departure, and since 2020 as co-creative director of Prada.
Simons seemingly thrives wherever he lands.

While at Jil Sander, Simons was approached
by costumier Antonella Cannarozzi to interpret her
ideas for Italian-language romance *I Am Love* (*Io sono
l'amore*, 2009). The result was a collection of new and
reconstructed garments to fit the unfussy couture of

moneyed Europe. *I Am Love* concentrates on the colourful blossoming of central character Emma Recchi (Tilda Swinton) as she embarks on an affair with a young lover and subsequently frees herself from well-bred Milanese society. Emma's fiery red dress, for example – a visual metaphor for her latent desire – was actually from Simons' Winter 2008 collection for Jil Sander. Originally in grey, Simons had the dress remade in red to fit narrative requirements. *I Am Love* features some of the most colour-specific costume design of any contemporary film in recent years.

Each item of clothing worn by Emma is intended to reflect sexual awakening and the rejection of her former life. Most interesting is that Tilda Swinton's carefully chosen wardrobe of unembellished shift dresses and plain knitwear, the entirety of which

p172 Tilda Swinton in *I Am Love* wearing Raf Simons for Jil Sander. Despite the obviously clean visual aesthetic, Simons does not view his output as 'minimalist'
—
p173 Swinton's red dress in *I Am Love* was originally grey, but costumier Antonella Cannarozzi requested that Simons dye it red to better fit the narrative

was provided by Simons and his team, was embraced so enthusiastically by fashion media as the ultimate in feminine sophistication. Yet within the context of the story, Emma is trapped by the inherent emptiness of these clothes and ultimately leaves her family behind to elope wearing a tracksuit top and baggy cotton pants. The film is derisive of a so-called feminine ideal and, as beautiful as Emma's perfectly coordinated ensembles are, rejects them in favour of bohemian comfort. It is probable that Simons spotted this irony from the outset. His role at Jil Sander was essentially to move the brand away from minimalism and provide a more innovative and commercial appeal. Simons's costumes are a reflection of the best of Jil Sander. In fact, despite a fawning press, *I Am Love* remains a fervently anti-fashion film.

Raf Simons's collaboration with Antonella Cannarozzi was harmonious and rewarding, even helping to score the costumier an Academy Award nomination – extremely rare for near-present-day clothing in film (*I Am Love* is set around 2000). Seeing his clothes build and adopt character away from the catwalk, even if it was not necessarily complimentary, impressed Simons. Cannarozzi's methodology for *I Am Love* was considered and restrained; she was not tempted to showcase the luxurious fashions surrounding her. For Cannarozzi, a costumier's role has always been function rather than flattery – dress the character not the actor.

In 2013 Raf Simons was signed to provide exclusive costumes for lead actresses Sigourney Weaver and Isabelle Huppert in *Body Art*, based on Don DeLillo's 124-page novella *The Body Artist*. Something akin to a ghost story, *The Body Artist* concerns a recently widowed woman drawn to a mystery inside the stark beach house where she resides. It was an ideal fit for Simons at Dior – a chance to open up a claustrophobic world with light, fresh designs reflecting his latest work at the house. However, Weaver and Huppert have now left the project and a new director has taken the reins, so it is unknown whether Simons will remain involved. Bearing in mind how much he enjoyed and learned from his experience with *I Am Love*, alongside his desire to tackle projects outside his comfort zone, he will almost certainly create for cinema again.

RALPH LAUREN

THE GREAT GATSBY (1974)
ANNIE HALL (1977)
MANHATTAN (1979)

Ralph Lauren looks at drawings in his 7th Avenue office in New York, 1977. Lauren's pioneering masculine, equestrian-inspired style set trends well into the eighties
—
p174 Robert Redford as Jay Gatsby in *The Great Gatsby*. Here Redford wears a suit made by Ralph Lauren and tailored to costumier Theoni V. Aldredge's specifications

Born in the Bronx, New York, into the humblest of upbringings during the tail end of the Great Depression, Ralph Lauren now commands an empire worth more than $6 billion. He fell in love with cinema at a young age, escaping into a fantasy world of wealth and style. This fuelled his passion for clothes and fine tailoring. Dapper Fred Astaire was one of his favourites – in essence an American dressed as a Savile Row English gent, but with a flair for the quirky (Astaire often used a tie instead of a belt when rehearsing, an idea he borrowed from his choreographer Hermes Pan). Since the seventies, when his business was thriving, Lauren has been associated with film, although not always in the most positive light. In actuality, every time his clothes have appeared on screen, it has caused controversy.

The problems began with *The Great Gatsby* in 1974, the third cinematic adaption of F. Scott Fitzgerald's novel, starring Robert Redford and Mia Farrow. Lauren was to be in direct contact with costume designer Theoni V. Aldredge, who was brought onto the production only two weeks before shooting; they were to collaborate together on the finished garments. After initially meeting with Aldredge, the two agreed on a visual template for menswear to be worn by Redford as Jay Gatsby. Aldredge wanted changes to the

Hardly any Ralph Lauren clothing is used in Annie Hall,
but the 'Lauren look' of thirties-inspired boxy silhouettes
is adopted by Diane Keaton's character throughout

suits Lauren suggested to better fit the story's twenties
setting and to use some different fabrics. Unfortunately,
Lauren failed to take Aldredge's suggestions into
account, and what he eventually provided was deemed
unsuitable by Aldredge. Only two Lauren suits were
worn by Redford in the finished picture, plus a selection
of shirts and ties chosen by Aldredge. For this minor
contribution, Lauren declared himself the costume
designer of the film, publically embellishing his involvement. This infuriated Aldredge, who threatened to sue
Lauren for misrepresenting his role. Aldredge went
on to win the Academy Award for costume design for
The Great Gatsby and notably left Lauren out of her
acceptance speech. It makes sense that the boy who
fell in love with the golden age of Hollywood would
aspire to be part of the industry. Make no bones about
it; Lauren wanted to win an Oscar. However, the only
way he could achieve this was to be a member of the
Costume Designers Guild. Public touting or even a
shared credit would not be enough. Understandably,
after *The Great Gatsby*, Lauren's movie career became
somewhat quieter.

Ralph Lauren's signature look is inspired by
the past, mainly the thirties, with relaxed yet smart
tailoring at the forefront. Wide-leg trousers, wide-lapel
suits, country tweeds, and later, following the debut of

his famous polo shirt with polo player insignia, a preppy
vibe aimed at a younger market. Lauren's first men's
line was launched in 1968 as 'Polo Fashions'. Lauren
really made his name with men's ties. He stood out with
a radical approach in the mid-sixties when everything
was skinny and straight by producing a tie that pre-
dates the kipper in terms of width, but is far less
cartoonish; this was more like the gangster aesthetic of
Prohibition Chicago. When director Woody Allen's land-
mark gender comedy *Annie Hall* was released in 1977,
it sparked an unlikely revival of Lauren's 'big tie' – this
time exclusively worn by women.

For the title character of Annie, Diane Keaton
was allowed to pick her own clothing. Precisely how
she wore these outfits and when was down to the film's
costume designer Ruth Morley. Annie is not native to
Allen's beloved New York; she is a Midwesterner, rather
intimidated by the pseudo-intellectual crowd now surrounding her. Her clothes echo this feeling of disenfran-
chisement. She stands out in the one way she knows
she can: her individuality. Ironically, in real life this
'individuality' was sparked by artistic ladies Keaton had
observed living in SoHo. Only a small portion of what
Keaton wears in *Annie Hall* was made by Ralph Lauren,
and this was part of her personal wardrobe rather
than provided specifically for the film. Again, though

Woody Allen chose Ralph Lauren to costume him
for *Manhattan* and has since remained a loyal fan

perhaps with less vigour, Lauren was keen to take credit for 'dressing' the main star of a major Hollywood movie, and again the costume designer took umbrage. Ruth Morley, like Theoni Aldredge, threatened to sue Lauren for overinflating his involvement. Nonetheless, praise must be heaped upon Keaton's canny eye for spotting an upcoming trend of traditionally masculine attire appropriated for a female market. This is something that made Lauren's name too, as much a part of his legacy as polo shirts and pinstriped suits. His waistcoats, slacks and wide neckties, donned by Keaton and copied the world over, are now capsule items in his womenswear. Lauren may not have dressed Annie Hall, but his look defined her.

    Ralph Lauren went on to provide Woody Allen's own costumes – a uniform mix of casual check shirts, natural-waist trousers and tweed sports jacket – as anxious writer Isaac in *Manhattan* (1979). Again Lauren solidified a classic look in cinema, and one that would be associated with the actor as much as the character he played. Decades later, Allen would direct Owen Wilson as anxious writer Gil in *Midnight in Paris* (2011), a role he would definitely have taken in his younger days. And what does Wilson wear in the film? Casual check shirts, natural-waist trousers and tweed sports jacket, of course.

Lauren's house style, particularly his younger-market menswear, is often compared to designer Tommy Hilfiger. It is considered very 'American' – sporty, college inspired, layered and usually modelled by a beefcake boy in a popped collar. However, unlike Hilfiger, who provided all costumes for the teen characters in high-school horror *The Faculty* (1998), Lauren has never supplied clothes for a whole movie. Yet despite this he is still persistently linked to film not only as someone who shaped two of the most celebrated costume movies of the seventies, but also as a fan. He loves cinema and, controversially or otherwise, has left an indelible mark on its sartorial history.

RODARTE

BLACK SWAN (2010)

Costume sketch for *Black Swan* by Amy Westcott. The core ballet costumes in the film were designed by Zack Brown

—

p178 Tutu worn by Natalie Portman in *Black Swan*. The original concept for the 'powder puff' tutu actually came from New York City Ballet costumier Barbara Karinska

The inclusion of Rodarte on any list of designer fashion on film is going to be controversial. After the release of *Black Swan* (2010), their only feature credit to date, the brand found itself at the centre of a very public discussion regarding their exact role in the project.

Rodarte are the sister duo Laura and Kate Mulleavy. Though based in Los Angeles, they became darlings of the New York fashion scene following their baroque-influenced 2005 collection, impressing the likes of *Vogue* editor-in-chief Anna Wintour. Rodarte were no strangers to the world of ballet when they signed on to assist, having made a *Swan Lake*–inspired dress of their own in 2007. Moreover, the wrapped, bandage-like style of their earliest work mirrored the layering effect commonly seen in dance studios. The hiring of Rodarte was embraced by star Natalie Portman, who was a friend and fan of the sisters' clothes, having worn them at several public events. Director Darren Aronofsky wanted a happy and comfortable leading lady, so their inclusion must have seemed a no-brainer from his point of view.

Black Swan is centred on virginal New York ballet dancer Nina's (Natalie Portman) sexual and psychological awakening. Nina must probe the dark side of her soul to successfully portray the Black Swan character in

a career-making production of *Swan Lake*. Most of the costumes Nina sports are warm-up ensembles and day attire, but for the production itself, she wears intricate custom-designed tutus as the White and Black Swan.

According to the costume designer of *Black Swan*, Amy Westcott, Rodarte only jumped on board the publicity machine after they discovered the film was destined to be a hit. Westcott was also unhappy that at no point did Rodarte mention her name during their many interviews as 'the costume designers of *Black Swan*'. As Westcott has stressed, Rodarte's input was part of a team effort, along with Westcott herself and director Darren Aronofsky. On the other hand, Rodarte were neither listed in the opening titles of *Black Swan*, nor were they eligible for official recognition during awards season, in accordance with the Costume Designers Guild regulations (Rodarte not being members).

How the Rodarte collaboration functioned was in essence straightforward. Costume design for the film began several months before shooting. Westcott worked closely with Aronofsky and the film's production designer and director of photography to ensure a cohesive visual balance. Everything had to be in tune to reflect Nina's journey and Aronofsky's vision. Aronofsky asked Westcott to contact Rodarte

officially about working together on the ballet costumes. Westcott was impressed by the sisters' Spring/Summer 2010 collection, which followed the theme of a girl who turns into a vulture, something that seemed an appropriate fit for the *Swan Lake* production at the end of the film. Rodarte's involvement was eventually limited to seven of the final ballet tutus, designed alongside Westcott and Aronofsky. Outfits for the core dancers were conceived and created by Zack Brown for American Ballet Theater. All other costumes were designed and/or sourced, altered and created by Amy Westcott and her team.

The *Swan Lake* tutus for *Black Swan* are spectacular creations. Their feathered grace makes for an awe-inspiring last act. They are costumes within a costume, designed to convey visually the internal struggle of Nina and that of her character on stage – which, as it tragically turns out, are one and the same. Colour is significant in the movie, too. Nina's everyday ensembles reflect the gradual darkening of her spirit as the Black Swan envelopes her mind and body. The effect is subtle but readable, and a textbook example of how costume design can intentionally enhance narrative. Nina's stage costumes are different; they are deliberately intended to wow both in and out of context. Rodarte have a reputation for being fastidious –

p180 left Rodarte's Spring/Summer 2010 collection,
inspired by Death Valley and vultures, impressed costume
designer Amy Westcott

—

p180 right Costume sketch for *Black Swan* by
Amy Westcott

—

p181 The white swan tutu for *Black Swan* – a collaboration
between costume designer Amy Westcott, director Darren
Aronofsky and Rodarte

a trait that served them well when it came to tackling
the couture art of designing a tutu, though may have
caused friction within the fast-paced and pragmatic
world of film-making.

Despite the controversy concerning their
involvement, Rodarte entered the costume arena
again after *Black Swan*, designing the costumes for
the Los Angeles Philharmonic's 2012 production of
Don Giovanni. The costumes of *Black Swan*, meanwhile,
took home a BAFTA nomination and Costume Designers
Guild award for Amy Westcott, minus any public
endorsement of Rodarte's contribution.

SALVATORE FERRAGAMO

THE POSTMAN ALWAYS RINGS TWICE (1946)

AUSTRALIA (2008)

RUSH (2013)

Salvatore Ferragamo in front of various celebrities' shoe forms, from Lauren Bacall to Gloria Swanson, 1956

—

p182 Nicole Kidman in Salvatore Ferragamo leather gloves for *Australia*. Ferragamo also produced a tie-in pair of red velvet gloves similar to those seen on Kidman in the film

A style behemoth that now extends to clothes, eye-wear, watches and accessories, once upon a time Salvatore Ferragamo was shoes only – the finest shoes in the world. Italian-born Salvatore had already crafted footwear for his family before emigrating to America in 1914 and setting up his own workshop. He produced made-to-measure, expensive shoes, which of course made them exclusive. Coupled with their Mezzogiorno heritage, this also made them fashionable in Hollywood. The company thrived after World War II, with clients including all major personalities of the era, such as Marilyn Monroe, Sophia Loren, Audrey Hepburn and the First Lady of Argentina, Eva Perón. Savvy Ferragamo even produced a shoe called the 'Audrey' to trade off their association with the actress.

Ferragamo footwear was regularly used in front of the camera too, seen in *The Ten Commandments* (1923; director Cecil B. DeMille asked Ferragamo to make 12,000 pairs of sandals for the film), *Mildred Pierce* (1945) and *Some Like it Hot* (1959), among many others. Lana Turner specifically requested her own Ferragamo open-toe sandals be remade for her role as femme fatale wife Cora in *The Postman Always Rings Twice* (1946).

Lana Turner's original sandals were blue suede, but here are recreated in white to fit her character's overall colour palette; supposedly innocent, but in truth scheming. In one scene Cora lays on a sofa buffing her shoes like they are fingernails; keeping them primed to dig into thuggish drifter Frank ('You won't find anything cheap around here', Cora sneers). She also sports a pair of black suede stilettos and white open-toe wedges, though neither of these are Ferragamo. Ironic, as he is generally seen as inventor of the wedge style, or at the least its champion. The costume designer for *The Postman Always Rings Twice*, Irene, was not concerned that Turner's sandals would date; they were popular towards the end of the thirties, as were open-toe slippers, and remained this way throughout the following decade. Incidentally, Ferragamo himself is widely cited as the creator of Judy Garland's sparkling ruby red slippers as Dorothy in *The Wizard of Oz*, but there is no evidence that this is the case. Adrian is credited costumier and the design originated entirely from him.

Ferragamo are eager to promote their involvement in cinema, with an entire section devoted to film on their website. For *Evita* (1996), costume designer Penny Rose selected shoes from Ferragamo's archives for Madonna to wear as Eva Perón, including a dramatic red suede open-toe sandal. In real life, Perón reputedly had Ferragamo shoes made to match all of her outfits. Most of the brand's work has been contemporary, yet some of their most famous footwear was created for *Ever After: A Cinderella Story* (1998), a postmodern historical take on the Grimm fairy tale. The handmade satin, muslin and Swarovski-covered slippers seen on Drew Barrymore as Danielle de Barbarac (aka Cinderella) were sold as custom-made replicas in boutiques for $2,500.

Australia (2008) is essentially 'Ferragamo the movie'. Dressed with spectacular attention to detail by Catherine Martin, Nicole Kidman wears Ferragamo leather gloves and footwear as fish-out-of-water Lady Sarah Ashley. Ferragamo produced 18 separate shoe variations, 73 pairs in total. Martin worked in tandem with Ferragamo to create styles that would suit the story's late-thirties/early-forties setting without becoming bogged down in history. *Australia* is far from a documentary, so creative licence was taken where necessary: for example, Kidman's shoes are stilettos rather than period-accurate wedges. Her red velvet and stingray examples were available to purchase as a $950 tie-in, as were a pair of matching velvet gloves. Similarly, Martin asked R.M. Williams to provide boots for Hugh Jackman's rough and ready Drover. These alliances are a speciality for Martin, who also employed Prada to make Kidman's extravagant luggage set in the movie. (She would go on to work extensively with Prada again for *The Great Gatsby*, 2013; see page 166).

In seventies-set true-life drama *Rush* (2013), Ferragamo was used by costume designer Julian Day to visually distinguish its racing-driver protagonists.

James Hunt (Chris Hemsworth) and his partner wear Gucci to express their brazenness (see page 84), while Niki Lauda (Daniel Brühl) and his wife Marlene (Alexandra Maria Lara) are represented by more demure Ferragamo. Day had Ferragamo clothing recreated directly from their archive. A close-up of Brühl's dark brown and tan two-tone fringed loafer (classic seventies Ferragamo) provides his character with a rare flash of attitude. This works perfectly in context as it is the first time we ever see him show off. Ferragamo is also featured as a trackside billboard ad, something that is not afforded their opposite number, Gucci. Unfortunately it seems that the creative head of Ferragamo, Massimiliano Giornetti, has been content to accept credit for designing all of Brühl and Lara's costumes in *Rush*, with scant mention of Day. A lack of recognition can ultimately damage a successful fashion/costume relationship, and while the fault may lie on either side, it is often the personalities in the fashion industry who are prone to claiming the collective glory.

Salvatore Ferragamo died in 1960. He saw his company through its zenith as the choice of red-carpet footwear for those in the public eye. Nonetheless, as an all-encompassing brand there is still much to expect from Ferragamo in front of the camera. The name represents bygone eras of nostalgic indulgence, which costume designers cannot resist tapping into.

p184 Lana Turner's white shoes for *The Postman Always Rings Twice* were by Ferragamo, based on a pair that had been made for her by the brand back in 1939. Her costumes were by Irene Lentz (see page 114)

—

p185 top Daniel Brühl in costume for *Rush*. His clothing in the film was by costumier Julian Day, based on the archival collections of Ferragamo

—

p185 bottom Stingray and red velvet sandals made by Salvatore Ferragamo and worn by Nicole Kidman in *Australia*

STELLA MCCARTNEY

SKY CAPTAIN AND THE WORLD OF TOMORROW (2004)

Costume sketch by Kevin Conran for Gwyneth Paltrow's character Polly Perkins in *Sky Captain and the World of Tomorrow*

—

p186 Stella McCartney made Gwyneth Paltrow's tweed suit for *Sky Captain and the World of Tomorrow* based on original sketches by costume designer Kevin Conran

S tella McCartney hasn't made many costumes for film or television, and by all accounts has never shown much interest in working outside of fashion. Yet what she has produced is inventive and memorable.

Apart from the obligatory *Sex and the City* movie contribution, an off-the-rack striped silver blouse for Sarah Jessica Parker, McCartney's main input to cinema has been a solitary moss-green tweed skirt suit. Worn by Gwyneth Paltrow as ace reporter Polly Perkins in *Sky Captain and the World of Tomorrow* (2004), this late-thirties pseudo-period garment was not necessarily something that McCartney ever wanted to become involved in, but was more a negotiating ploy on the part of the film's producers. The intention was to entice Paltrow to join the production by asking her good friend and future fashion collaborator to design the costumes. McCartney did not have the time or inclination to design for an entire movie, but she did agree to make Paltrow's primary ensemble, based on an original sketch by costume designer Kevin Conran. The entire look of *Sky Captain* was illustrated early in pre-production because the whole film was to be rendered via computer-generated imagery (CGI). In fact, the actors, costumes and props were the only non-CGI elements. *Sky Captain* was the first feature of this type ever made.

Polly gets a charm bracelet from Smooth Captain — moon, stars, P-40 etc...

of course he should have also given one to Frankie...

Kevin Conran's original skirt suit was more realistic in terms of what a reporter on Polly's salary could afford. Certainly the gold 'PP' belt buckle was added by Stella McCartney. Essentially Polly is wearing a custom-made designer suit with her initials on the front. Polly stands out as somebody special, or more accurately, wealthy, but in fact she is neither – and this is her supposed charm. Yet *Sky Captain* is an alternative timeline of the thirties, featuring giant robots attacking Manhattan, so who is to say what is realistic in terms of design? As far as audiences are concerned, Polly's outlandish suit with its PP buckle, bib-front bodice and leg-of-mutton sleeves, topped with slanted fedora, is simply a unique creative touch. All of the other costumes in *Sky Captain* were designed and created by Kevin Conran, including Paltrow's 'woolly mammoth' coat, Jude Law's Irvin-inspired flight jacket, and Angelina Jolie's skintight RAF outfit.

Stella McCartney's only other involvement with cinema, so far, was for Madonna's time-hopping drama *W.E.* (2011), which centres on the romantic relationship between socialite Wallis Simpson and King Edward VIII.

In this instance, McCartney's input was limited to two blink-and-you-will-miss-them garments. The ensemble generally credited to McCartney is that worn by Wally (Abbie Cornish) as she visits the Sotheby's estate sale. This was, in fact, created by the film's costume designer Arianne Phillips. McCartney made only an under-slip and a dressing gown – working from real-life photographs of Wallis Simpson given to her by Phillips – which was used on screen as a background prop.

When she arrived on the fashion scene as a graduate of Central Saint Martins in 1995, Stella McCartney struggled to be taken seriously. Predictable accusations of trading on her famous father's name became even more vehement when she succeeded Karl Lagerfeld as creative director of Chloé in 1997. Her first collection was a proto-punk mash-up strewn with cockney rhyming slang. But McCartney worked hard to make her mark, ironically not by carving out a personal style at all but by refusing to conform to one. If she can – or more importantly, if she wants to – channel this same eclectic spirit into the realm of costume design, there is no reason why we should not hear from her again.

p188 Kevin Conran's sketches of the character Polly Perkins in *Sky Captain and the World of Tomorrow* drove the development of Gwyneth Paltrow's costumes for the film

—

p189 top Stella McCartney's tweed suit for Gwyneth Paltrow with leg-of-mutton sleeves captures the look of *Sky Captain*'s thirties setting

—

p189 bottom Polly Perkins's gold 'PP' belt buckle was a creative touch added by Stella McCartney

TIZIANI

THE COMEDIANS (1967)
BOOM! (1968)

A sketch of new ideas from Tiziani, 1967. Although the brand's designs were not generally groundbreaking, their theatrical indulgence ensured an exclusive, and very wealthy, client base

—

p190 Elizabeth Taylor wearing a headdress created by Tiziani for *Boom!* This was the last collaboration up-and-coming Karl Lagerfeld would undertake with the house

'Tiziani Roma', 'Tiziani of Rome' or just plain 'Tiziani', the name was a lie. Tiziani was actually conceived and run by a Texas cowboy, while many of the clothes were manufactured in England. The house was a lie but far from a joke; counting among its clients such luminaries as Gina Lollobrigida and Elizabeth Taylor, it made some remarkably evocative gowns in the sixties and seventies. Thanks to an early association with one of the most famous contemporary designers of all time, Tiziani now survives as something far greater than a society brand.

Tiziani's founder was a man named Evan Richards. Couturier was last on the list of his many job titles, though he was a wily businessman. Realizing a Texas-owned fashion label would never make much of an impression on those with deep pockets, he dreamed up Tiziani as a variation on sixteenth-century Italian artist Titian. Image was everything. It worked too; Elizabeth Taylor actually thought his name was Evan Tiziani.

Elizabeth Taylor became a Tiziani client after deviating from Valentino couture in 1967 while shooting *The Taming of the Shrew*. Although he did not costume that particular film, Tiziani worked with Taylor several times during subsequent years, arguably personifying the actress during her second zenith. The unyielding

Tiziani designed for Elizabeth Taylor in *The Comedians*.
As with all Taylor films of the time, regardless of setting
and period, plummeting necklines were the real star

feminine beauty of fifties Taylor was vastly different from her more liberated, hippy sixties vibe, although no less enticing.

    Richards knew to surround himself with the best of the up and coming. As was the case with many of his contemporaries during their early careers, German-born designer Karl Lagerfeld went freelance for larger, more financially secure houses – in this instance, Tiziani. After a short period, Tiziani moved from couture to ready-to-wear, and Lagerfeld left the company to build his own label. Before his departure, though, Lagerfeld, known for adding finishing touches to Richards's designs, worked alongside Richards on costumes for several films. One of these films was *The Comedians* (1967).

    The Comedians was Taylor's third official on-screen collaboration with Tiziani. The film was set in contemporary Haiti but shot in West Africa, and director Peter Glenville was keen that her wardrobe be pastel to contrast with the location. Taylor plays Martha Pineda, the philandering wife of a diplomat, so required a uniform of stately gowns lightly influenced by the fashions of the day. Her skirts were marked at

one inch above the knee, though the actress preferred precisely an inch and a half, even if, as was the case with *Reflections in a Golden Eye* (1967, also Tiziani), which was set post-World War II, this hardly made them historically accurate. For further confirmation, see Taylor's ultra-plunging-cleavage dresses for *Cleopatra*. In any case, the palette for *The Comedians* was subdued, very early sixties, using lightweight tropical fabrics like shantung silk and linen. Taylor sports some huge hair in the film, which almost distracts from her costumes, though a patterned eau de nil wrap-over dress with V-neckline and long sleeves gathered into the cuff is a notable standout.

    One of the last projects that Lagerfeld had a hand in while he was with Tiziani was *Boom!* (1968). *Boom!* is a classic Taylor and Burton vanity project, based on a Tennessee Williams script from his own play. Taylor plays Flora 'Sissy' Goforth, lady of the manor, summering on a private island in the Sardinian sun, five marriages under her kimono sash and a fondness for setting her dogs on any casual callers. Her clothes, all by Tiziani (Richards with Karl Lagerfeld assisting), are a blend of mainly white, loose-fitting,

This 1966 striped, full-skirted silk evening dress by Tiziani features the type of lustrous, lavish fabric that Elizabeth Taylor's character in *The Comedians* craves

Detail of the elaborately embroidered Japanese-style kabuki gown made by Tiziani for Elizabeth Taylor in *Boom!* The gown was sold at auction in 2011

draped garments, such as a muumuu, kabuki costume, fur-trimmed robe, and pared-down sheath with matching oversized plastic sunglasses, and even trousers and tunic lined in Taylor's favourite purple. During the sequence when Noel Coward's character, 'the Witch of Capri', comes to dinner, himself attired in a tailored Douglas Hayward tuxedo, Sissy dons a jaw-dropping embroidered kabuki gown with oversized spiked head-dress (basically an elaborate turban) festooned with Bulgari jewels and ornate daisies. Sissy's infatuation with Japanese culture reaches back to the one man in her life that she loved. They would dress up in costume every day and threaten each other with knives and guns – it was their foreplay. Sissy has a damaged psyche, but not so cracked that uninvited visitor Chris Flanders (Burton) cannot see through it. She wears flamboyant clothing to create a facade, a distraction from any attempt to read the woman inside – superficially a bitter, angry bully. Really Sissy is just pining for lost love. During one scene the full extent of her wardrobe is revealed: literally dozens of dresses and kimonos to waft about in. She even forces Chris to don one of her black kimonos and a sword, because in her

mind it is the 'costume of a professional warrior'. As Sissy comes to battle with everybody, she wants those that fascinate her to stand a chance. The kabuki attire is not intended as an accurate copy – it is not colourful enough for a start – but it represents a late-sixties Westernized trend for reimagining clothing of foreign climes (Thea Porter was especially known for this).

Boom! was a brave role for Elizabeth Taylor because it is not difficult to imagine Sissy as a reflection of the actress in real life; a mesmerizingly beautiful woman, tough and demanding, but fragile enough to require complete control over her appearance. Tiziani made her look both comfortable and glamorous; he dressed the character and the star.

TOM FORD

QUANTUM OF SOLACE (2008)
SKYFALL (2012)
SPECTRE (2015)

Tom Ford directing *A Single Man,* 2009. Ford did not act as costume designer on the film, instead asking long-time friend Arianne Phillips to take on the role

—

p194 Daniel Craig wears a brown hopsack, single-breasted Tom Ford suit with double vents in *Quantum of Solace*

E ven on the strength of just one completed feature to date, it is possible that Tom Ford's skills as a film-maker might eventually outstrip those as a designer. What sets him apart is a comprehension of how clothes communicate – something that many fashion designers who dip their toes into cinema fail to grasp. Ford can, apparently effortlessly, blend visual splendour with that most fundamental requirement of costume design: conveying character. The costumes worn by George Falconer (Colin Firth) in early-sixties-set drama *A Single Man* (2009) reflect and support the tone of the film; one of emotional control – or lack thereof – and a precise, albeit knowingly stylized, manifestation of period.

Tom Ford acted as director and writer on *A Single Man* (adapted from the novel of the same name by Christopher Isherwood), but surprisingly not as costume designer. Although menswear bearing his name was used for George, overall costumier for the film was Ford's friend Arianne Phillips. Better known as Madonna's stylist, Phillips is also an accomplished costume designer, having worked on films such as *Walk the Line* (2005), *3:10 to Yuma* (2007) and recently, *W.E.* (2011). It was a perfect blend, making *A Single Man* one of the standout costume movies of that year. Phillips might have been costumier, but in her own words,

p196 Pinstriped Tom Ford suit worn by Daniel Craig for *Quantum of Solace* – James Bond's first Ford suit of the series
—
p197 top Charcoal Tom Ford suit with single vent worn by Daniel Craig in *Skyfall*. The suit is incredibly tight – hardly practical for a man in Bond's physical line of work
—
p197 bottom Blue overcheck Tom Ford suit with slanted hip pockets from *Spectre*. The suit was fitted so closely that different versions were required for different scenes, depending on the action

'he [Ford] made my work better'. Ford wanted to convey a language through clothes in a way that most directors are not overly interested in. The dark brown single-breasted suit and accompanying blazer worn by Colin Firth was manufactured to her specifications under Ford's own label. It also had a backstory created together by Phillips, Ford and Firth: George had the suit tailored for him on Savile Row in the fifties before he moved to America. That is why it is ever so slightly snug around the middle – a slight but significant detail, along with the two spaced buttons on George's jacket sleeves, a feature that is generally only seen on bespoke. Although a collaborative effort, Ford credits Arianne Phillips as the sole costume designer for the film.

Tom Ford's clothes are also well known for covering Daniel Craig's swollen muscles as 007 in three James Bond films (so far) – *Quantum of Solace*

(2008), *Skyfall* (2012) and *Spectre* (2015). It was costume designer Louise Frogley who saw the potential of putting Bond in a Tom Ford suit for *Quantum of Solace*. This was in 2007 – only one year after Ford had parted ways with Gucci to set up his own menswear label. Frogley appreciated Ford's clean, unfussy mantra, particularly where suits are concerned, bringing him onboard to provide 11 changes for Craig – suits and a shawl-collar cardigan.

Louise Frogley wanted the Tom Ford suits she had seen on the catwalk: slim but not overly contoured, with a longer than typical skirt. The suits Ford provided for *Quantum of Solace* are amongst the best Bond has ever worn in Craig's guise, perfectly fitting the actor's 42-inch chest with an enviable 10-inch drop. Excusing for a moment the ridiculous notion that Bond would find a perfectly tailored suit just hanging up in a locker, a midnight blue tuxedo with concave shoulders and low trouser rise is classic Tom Ford in terms of cut and fit.

The classic lines in *Quantum of Solace* are precisely why the suits provided by Ford for *Skyfall* are so peculiar in comparison. It is almost as though costume designer Jany Temime wanted the Tom Ford name but without a full understanding of what makes the cut of his suits special – essentially, they are ageless. Temime was not pressured to use Tom Ford on *Skyfall*, but a relationship of supply, demand and marketing was in place. What we see in the movie are Temime's sketches interpreted by Ford, as opposed to the suits in *Quantum of Solace*, which were supplied by and based on the requirements of Louise Frogley but not her own designs. As a result, the classic Tom Ford look was somewhat lost in translation. Even though Ford himself was steering away from the more conventional *Quantum* look of 2008 to slimmer-cut styles, the suits seen on Daniel Craig in *Skyfall* are so tight and short at times that he seems borderline uncomfortable.

In *Spectre* (2015), Craig's suits were on the very edge between ultra-body-hugging and too small. This was more a choice of Jany Temime, however, because the suits themselves are perfectly cut to contour the body with a slim but correctly fitting silhouette. Ford has released the entire screen-accurate *Spectre* collection into his stores; practically everything Tom Ford from the movie is there. The suits, featuring a notched lapel and two-button fastening, actually fit better in real life when worn to the correct size. Incidentally, Daniel Craig's suits in *Spectre* are not the incorrect size but were retro-tailored to fit closer to his body, sometimes in several versions according to different requirements: for example, fight scene suits sport longer arms so they do not disappear past Craig's elbow when throwing a punch. A Tom Ford suit is one of the most desirable garments in the world; to remain that way on screen, Ford clearly needs to retain as much creative control as possible. After all, the greatest secret agent in the world wears his name.

TRAVIS BANTON

MOROCCO (1930)
SHANGHAI EXPRESS (1932)
MY MAN GODFREY (1936)

Travis Banton showing sketches to Marlene Dietrich, mid-1930s
—
p198 Marlene Dietrich in top hat and tuxedo for *Morocco*, an ensemble designed and put together by Travis Banton that became her signature look

It is tricky to ascertain exactly why Travis Banton is not a more renowned name in the costume design archives; possibly because his most prolific era, the thirties, involved a considerable amount of churned-out studio quickies, which, unless they featured a major star, have not been remastered or rereleased for contemporary audiences. Moreover, although he started in fashion and remained a custom couturier after his stint in Hollywood, Banton did not produce his own label like contemporaries Gilbert Adrian or Howard Greer. Whatever the reason, his skills were recognized as among the best in the business. Banton's first film for Paramount Pictures was *The Dressmaker from Paris* (1925); he *was* the dressmaker from Paris. His clothes were so exquisite, so forward thinking, that he could even have designed in the French capital.

Throughout his career as chief designer for Paramount (1929–38, then freelance until his death in 1958), Travis Banton worked with all of cinema's great female stars, including Clara Bow, Marlene Dietrich, Ida Lupino, Carole Lombard and Nancy Carroll. Despite considerable studio backing, Banton struggled to deal with the diva attitude exhibited by the more bankable actresses. Carroll unleashed a torrent of abuse and tears over a black lace gown Banton had made for *The Dance of Life* (1929), her director Edward Sutherland

Marlene Dietrich adjusts her bow tie in *Morocco*. In the late twenties (when *Morocco* is set), white-tie formal attire was a strict dress code worn only by men

describing it as 'unwearable'. Indeed the dress was unwearable – because she had it on backwards. This sort of self-indulgent behaviour was tolerated, with Carroll especially known for being one of the most demanding divas who ever lived, but Banton was still revered among those with whom he collaborated. Edith Head – the most famous costume designer of all time – was an assistant to Banton at Paramount and paid tribute to his astounding ability to drive and inspire those around him. Banton's style was all opulence: generally draped gowns cut on the bias in only the most lustrous fabrics. His movies were expensive, but they looked far more so. Banton had been an apprentice dressmaker for New York boutique Madame Frances, and this is what Hollywood hired him for: dresses, coats, hats and scarves so extravagantly beautiful that in real life they could only ever exist for the chosen few.

Nonetheless, for Marlene Dietrich's first film in Hollywood, *Morocco* (1930), Banton eschewed the era's more obvious glamour to craft a controversial indelible image in the history of cinema. Dietrich plays nightclub singer Amy Jolly, seen for only the second time wearing

white-tie formal attire for men: black tailcoat, black trousers, white wing-collar shirt, white dress waistcoat with white bow tie, white silk pocket square and black top hat (Dietrich also sports a top hat in *The Blue Angel*, 1930, generally regarded as her breakthrough movie). This ensemble was frequently seen in gentlemen's evening-wear before adoption of the then semiformal and now formal tuxedo jacket. Of course this outfit would not be worn by women, even a risqué entertainer such as Amy; moreover, Amy actually kisses another woman while performing. It was an awkward attraction for those who defined sexuality via strict adherence to gender models. However the iconic *Morocco* portrait of Dietrich in a cocked top hat holding a cigarette is now visual shorthand for androgyny in fashion and culture; Banton's costume defined an entire identity.

Banton and Dietrich made many films together, the third of which, *Shanghai Express* (1932), was influential in maintaining Dietrich's angular, raven-like look initiated in *Morocco*. By this juncture, their working relationship was intense and co-dependent. Make no mistake, Dietrich created costumes alongside Banton, putting in long hours of fitting and refitting until every

Banton's costumes for Dietrich in *Shanghai Express* were
designed to compound the exoticism of the film's locale

detail was perfect. The black cock feathers festooning Dietrich's most famous ensemble as Shanghai Lily were entirely her suggestion. Costumier and actress together made Lily a mysterious, hovering presence; whether she was predator or prey was unclear.

    Not all Banton's relationships with leading ladies were as harmonious as with Dietrich, however. Apart from Nancy Carroll's temper tantrum, Banton also had a legendary run-in with Claudette Colbert during the making of *Cleopatra* (1934). Conflicting versions of the story exist, but all revolve around Colbert's obsessive control of her own image. She reputedly vetoed every ensemble designed by director Cecil B. DeMille's own costume department, so Banton was brought onboard at the last minute. He had only 24 hours before shooting began to recreate Colbert's entire wardrobe as the bewitching Macedonian queen. Depending on which anecdotes you believe, she either accepted Banton's daily redesigned costumes – with desired emphasis on her bosom to distract from a supposedly thickening middle (she was tiny) – or marched off to her dressing room and refused to come out unless they were remade yet again. Whatever the process, the result did kick-start an off-screen trend for all things Egyptian: in Los Angeles, bias-cut gold lamé gowns, scarab headdresses and broad 'Egyptian collar' dresses were popping up at

all the right parties. Even under the gun, Banton could still churn out incredible costumes that, though owing practically nothing to the period in which the film was set, created their own quasi-ethnic fashion genre.

    My Man Godfrey (1936), set during the Great Depression, features a Travis Banton ensemble so renowned it has been restored and displayed in the touring Hollywood Costume exhibition. In this biting satire of moneyed 'nitwits' – a hangover from *The Great Gatsby* – Carole Lombard plays Irene, a well-meaning but clueless party girl who hires 'forgotten man' Godfrey (William Powell) to be her family's butler. Banton designed exclusively for Lombard, with his assistant Edith Head likely providing costumes for the rest of the female cast – with particular attention paid to seductive viper Cornelia (Gail Patrick), Irene's sister. The first dress worn by Lombard as Irene as she stands in a city dump surrounded by ash and tin cans talking to bemused tramp Godfrey is the one fêted in Hollywood Costume. Abruptly contrasting with Irene's physical environment, the dress is constructed of glass bugle beads stitched to silk georgette with matching duster jacket, a huge sapphire jewel at the jacket neckline. The fabric drapes and shimmers, giving Irene the appearance of a cosmonaut standing on another planet. This is an alien world to her, and she remains unfazed. This impresses

p202 left Claudette Colbert in a Travis Banton gown and white fox-fur coat, 1935. Colbert certainly gave Banton some costuming headaches; she was a renowned Hollywood diva known for making ludicrous on-set demands

—

p202 right Marlene Dietrich in a brown and beige suit, with a lynx-trimmed beige wool cape by Travis Banton, 1936. Dietrich was far more than the designer's muse; she was his collaborator

—

p203 Carole Lombard (left) wearing gold harem pants for *My Man Godfrey*. Travis Banton designed for Lombard both on and off screen

Godfrey despite her hilariously unsuitable attire. The dress was so heavy that it needed to be displayed in a 'lounging' position for Hollywood Costume (not a position that Lombard adopts while wearing it in the film), otherwise stress on the fragile seams would have been too great. The blue sapphire jewel was remade and inserted into the outfit as a colourful centrepiece, which would have been lost on viewers of the black-and-white movie. Irene is light to her sister Cornelia's dark at this point, a differentiation that shifts via costume as the story moves forward. Irene wears harem pants (pyjamas) and even a jumpsuit for the last act.

The harem pants reflected an art deco pre-occupation with the exotic. Banton has incorporated this facet into costume before, designing for Anna May Wong in *Shanghai Express*, notably a black silk evening dress with sequined dragon motif outwardly based on the Chinese one-piece cheongsam. When Travis Banton left Paramount to return to fashion design, he continued to create spectacular gowns for the privileged few – in essence, the real-life cast of *My Man Godfrey*.

VERA WANG

FIRST DAUGHTER (2004)
BRIDE WARS (2009)

Vera Wang at the *Vogue* magazine Fashion Fund Awards, 2015. Before becoming a designer, Wang was senior fashion editor for *Vogue*

—

p204 Anne Hathaway and Kate Hudson both wore Vera Wang gowns for *Bride Wars*, the contrasting styles representing their characters' very different personalities

The Vera Wang wedding dress – featured in several TV shows and movies since the early nineties – is the last word in lavishness. So much so that both the clashing protagonists of *Bride Wars* (2009) each wear a Vera Wang gown as they literally wrestle their friendship to the ground. Vera Wang is a costume designer of sorts, having created NFL cheerleading uniforms and leotards for figure skaters Nancy Kerrigan and Michelle Kwan. It is also worth noting that Wang was almost an Olympic-level skater herself before entering the world of fashion as an editor at *Vogue* magazine; this was followed by two years designing for Ralph Lauren before eventually opening her own wedding boutique in 1990. Though Wang is also known for her ready-to-wear women's collections, it is her wedding gowns that have had the most impact on screen.

Vera Wang was one of stylist Patricia Field's regularly featured labels on the show *Sex and the City* (1998–2004), specifically as wedding attire for Charlotte (Kristen Davis). It is hardly surprising, either, that the first dress Carrie (Sarah Jessica Parker) flaunts for a *Vogue* wedding shoot in the first *Sex and the City* movie (2008) is couture Vera Wang (a variation on her 'Eleanor' gown). Showcasing a tulle feathered skirt and floral stitched bodice, it is effortlessly absurd, and, like a huge floral bouquet, utterly divine.

Wang also takes credit for 'gowns' in *First Daughter* (2004). The film is a romantic fairy tale about the American president's daughter Samantha (Katie Holmes), allowed to leave her walled-up kingdom of the White House for the first time as she attends college. Samantha is impassive and straight-laced, distinguished from other students both by her extremely privileged background and by her surprisingly conservative wardrobe of light blue and white shirts, an occasional beige trench and shapeless black trousers. On state occasions, however, she is America's princess, dressed majestically in Vera Wang, with heavy, almost self-supporting skirts flowing from a fitted bodice, a silhouette reminiscent of early fifties Christian Dior. One dress in particular – a pink silk chiffon with matching wrap, gloves and sash – gives the illusion that Samantha glides rather than walks. The elitism of a Vera is echoed in television drama *The West Wing* (1999–2006), in which an episode is entitled 'The Black Vera Wang', as if to mark the significance of character C.J. (Alison Janney) choosing to wear one – the only dress for those who need to drop a name and garner instant gasps from those around them.

But it is the 2009 film *Bride Wars* that represents Vera Wang's most publicized work. The film, set in New York, is a comedy about two brides-to-be, lifelong friends Liv (Kate Hudson) and Emma (Anne Hathaway), attempting to sabotage each other's

p206 top Vera Wang designed all the evening gowns worn by Katie Holmes in *First Daughter*

—

p206 bottom Kate Hudson wearing a Vera Wang wedding dress for *Bride Wars*. Costume designer Karen Patch added additional train to Wang's dress so it could be torn off during the brawl scene

—

p207 A green trench coat worn by Anne Hathaway and designed by Vera Wang (Lavender label) in *Bride Wars*. Kate Hudson's trench is by Burberry

'perfect' wedding. Both girls are different at heart: Liv is a pushy go-getting lawyer, Emma a meek middle-school teacher. Both, however, are equally obsessed with the validity of a label-driven existence. For example, Liv buys Emma a blouse, but it is not just a blouse, it's a 'Dolce blouse'. Before their friendship turns sour, the girls go shopping for wedding dresses and immediately become entranced with a 'Vera' of 'Lace bodice, basque waist, ten-layer tulle'. It is the epitome of wedding dress chic. Although Emma spots the dress, Liv jumps in and buys it, but not before a warning from the bitchy sales assistant: 'You don't alter a Vera to fit you, you alter yourself to fit a Vera.' The perceived exclusivity of an opulent wedding gown comes at a price. Emma, on a more modest budget than Liv, eventually wears her mother's wedding dress instead – also a Vera Wang, as it happens, though this is never acknowledged in the narrative, and would most likely make no sense if it were. Costume designer Karen Patch worked with Vera Wang to recreate both dresses from her own collection. Patch then altered the fabric, and added more train and a sash to Hudson's gown so they could be torn off during the girls' fight towards the end of the film. Both ensembles suggest the different personalities of the characters: Emma's gown is traditional and romantic, while Liv's is far grander and audacious. The 2009 collection dress worn by Hudson and modified by Patch was actually put back into Vera Wang stores this way. Real-life brides could buy the Bride Wars Wang/Patch gown for a mere $6,000.

Wang's ready-to-wear Lavender label also makes an appearance in *Bride Wars*, though with different connotations. Anne Hathaway sports a green Lavender trench coat, in contrast to Hudson's Burberry. The Wang piece was selected by Karen Patch to reflect Emma's limited means, with key pieces in her wardrobe – few but high quality.

Today, Vera Wang is more than just bridalwear, it is a lifestyle brand selling everything from stationery to bedding. For any woman aspiring to be the definitive, flawless cinematic bride, however, a Vera Wang wedding dress is compulsory.

VERSACE

KIKA (1993)
DIE ANOTHER DAY (2002)
CASINO ROYALE (2006)
THE COUNSELOR (2013)
THE WOLF OF WALL STREET (2013)

Gianni Versace sitting in front of a wall of sketches in his study, 1985. Versace was strongly influenced by Greek architecture, and often incorporated those forms and shapes into his designs
—
p208 Black evening gown with fishtail skirt, provided by Versace and worn by Eva Green in *Casino Royale*

Versace has always played with notions of 'taste', embracing the term and redefining what it means in terms of aesthetic beauty. Since founder Gianni's first independent collection in 1978, Versace has attempted to cross stylistic boundaries. Gianni was not simply running riot with a pair of scissors; he was a procurer of fine art, a classicist, and an expert in the evolution of garments from a historical perspective, particularly the evening gown. The Versace evening gown was go-to for celebrities aiming to nab column inches during the nineties. Elizabeth Hurley wore Gianni's revealing black 'safety pin' dress in 1994 (loaned as a favour to the actress, not bespoke) and immediately gained a movie career. Gianni took great pleasure in designing for the theatre, though never directly for film.

Gianni Versace was murdered in 1997, aged 51, his own life perhaps more sensational than any movie he could have contributed to. His sister Donatella was immediately appointed artistic director of the house. Even though there was no significant move towards cinema, Donatella shared her brother's nose for savvy PR and celebrity endorsement. Under her direction, Versace is more famous than it has ever been.

Gianni loved art, and he spent time with other creative types such as Madonna and Spanish filmmaker Pedro Almodóvar. In fact Almodóvar personally asked Gianni to contribute to his movie *Kika* (1993), a black-as-night satire of real life played as a farcical reality show. Although Jean Paul Gaultier specially designed ensembles for the part of tabloid TV presenter Andrea (Victoria Abril) in *Kika* (see page 122), all Versace's clothes were sourced from his then current collection. Gianni never visited the set or interacted with Gaultier; Almodóvar (along with costumier José María de Cossío) dressed the title character of Kika (Verónica Forqué) himself. Andrea is a hard-edged, embittered compulsive, the exact opposite of optimistic ray-of-sunshine Kika. Their attire reflects this distinction. Kika is sweet and engaging, a cheerful wannabe actress/make-up artist who bounces from one experience in her hectic life to the next. She slips off an orange acrylic sheepskin coat to reveal a pink sheath dress and then promptly gets to work applying foundation to a corpse, casually muttering about hoping to have sex that day. Almodóvar chose Versace for Kika's costumes because his collection embraced a burgeoning neo-hippie vibe. Kika's clothes are all brightly coloured, often clashing, polka-dotted and/or floral-patterned gypsy tops, tiered skirts and dresses – her bosom generally on the verge of spilling out in each. This prioritizing of the female form was Almodóvar's intention, and one that he has never been shy of embracing in his films. Andrea, debatably the villain of the piece, is strapped up in Gaultier's pseudo bondage attire (exposed fake breasts notwithstanding), but Kika is embraced as a beautifully bare free spirit. Apart from the pink sheath with triple shoulder straps – typical Versace of the era – most of Kika's costumes are less about the designer and more about her character. It just so happens they were made by Versace; the silhouette says more about her than the label does.

Neither Gianni or (to date) Donatella have acted as costume designers on any movie, though Gianni was approached to provide concepts for the 1995 interpretation of comic book *Judge Dredd* – possibly because the Versace line throughout history is outwardly similar to Dredd's uniform: shiny and gold, heavily accessorized with a gigantic belt and shoulder armour, and just a mite camp. However, Gianni's own sketches for Dredd were deemed an embellished codpiece too far and ultimately rejected. In the end, costume design for the film fell to Emma Porteous.

Costumier Lindy Hemming has used product placement many times, having built strong relationships with designers during her lengthy career. She chose Versace for several of Halle Berry's outfits as secret agent Giacinta 'Jinx' Johnson in *Die Another Day* (2002). Hemming is a firm believer in collaborations with fashion and luxury goods houses, but only if they fulfil her requirements. Without these relationships she would not have the budget to clothe specific characters as we expect to see them. Hemming obtained lookbooks from Versace for their upcoming collections, believing the brand to be a perfect match for Jinx's

p210 top Verónica Forqué (right) wearing cheerfully clashing Versace prints in *Kika*

—

p210 bottom Halle Berry as Jinx in *Die Another Day*. Under instructions from Lindy Hemming, Versace remade the originally yellow dress in pink to align with Berry's character

—

p211 left Javier Bardem in *The Counselor*. His shirt was shopped by costume designer Janty Yates from Versace's 1995 collection

—

p211 right Beaded halterneck top worn by Margot Robbie in *The Wolf of Wall Street*: loud, insubstantial and a bit gaudy – all facets of her character

fiery personality. She found a yellow dress covered in Swarovski crystals that was ideal for the film's 'Ice Palace' party sequence. Versace agreed to remake the dress in cyclamen pink, which was Jinx's dedicated colour, and provided duplicates to use during the action sequences. Another Versace ensemble is Jinx's chocolate leather fringed skirt and jacket, worn for her arrival scene at the Ice Palace, a combo that Hemming found while trawling designer boutiques.

Hemming returned to Versace for *Casino Royale* (2006). They agreed to make several copies of the black silk jersey dress Eva Green's character, Vesper Lynd, wears for her second night at the Montenegro poker game. Bond, or more precisely Bond girls, and Versace have long been a good fit.

A Versace character is a visually memorable one, and that is why costumiers use the brand. Janty Yates dressed gaudy gangster Reiner (Javier Bardem) in a 1995 *barocco* butterfly-print silk shirt and green Belstaff moto leather jacket for *The Counselor* (2013). He, like Gianni, is a man who celebrates bad taste – fine fabrics in wild prints and lurid tones.

Costume designer Sandy Powell used Versace for trophy wife Naomi Lapaglia (Margot Robbie) in *The Wolf of Wall Street* (2013), this time focusing on its reputation as the yuppie brand of choice during the nineties. Versace's early nineties seqined halter sets an outrageous tone, but Powell's favourite costume

was Naomi's 'Super Girl' ensemble of cropped black leather jacket covered in gilt, black leggings, Versace sunglasses and Medusa logo boots. This idea of sporting one designer top to toe – even more so, one as recognizable as Versace – is very nouveau riche, ideally suiting conceited princess Naomi.

As a shopped couture label, what it means to wear Versace on screen is a vital component of character; it allows us, in mere seconds, to read someone from the outside in.

VIVIENNE WESTWOOD

TWENTY-ONE (1991)
LEAVING LAS VEGAS (1995)
SEX AND THE CITY (2008)
MUPPETS MOST WANTED (2014)

Vivienne Westwood at her Spring/Summer 2016 Red Label show, London Fashion Week. Note the argyle pattern on her sleeve; Westwood has long been a devotee of Scottish clan tartan

—

p212 Elisabeth Shue wearing a bustier provided by Vivienne Westwood in *Leaving Las Vegas*

Vivienne Westwood is one of the most important fashion designers of all time because she is always pushing boundaries, always interested in new culture, and always engaged with the times. Even so, we have not seen many of her creations on screen. Westwood began work as costumier on a stalled project featuring the Sex Pistols, and she did contribute a few pieces to Patsy Kensit's wardrobe in *Twenty-One* (1991). Frankly though, and by her own admission, she does not even go to the cinema.

Punk, that eternally significant movement of seditious slogans and tartan pants held together by safety pins, made Westwood's name. But by the late seventies, Westwood was already moving on. Punk was a political way of dressing, or it certainly began that way – a response to economic downturn and the incessantly upbeat tempo of disco. The world via London was ready to be depressed. Westwood tackled buffalo style and pirate wear in the early eighties, before becoming obsessed around 1987 with eighteenth-century costume, and one garment in particular – the corset. An extremely important part of history, with subtextual meaning well beyond its function, the corset was designed to slim the waist and hips way beyond their natural state. This allowed the blooming of colossal skirts and squishing of breasts up to the wearer's chin, which at various points during the seventeenth and eighteenth century was the height of fashion. Westwood reworked the corset for a contemporary market, replacing traditional tight lacing with a zip, reducing the amount of structural boning and elongating the classic V-shaped bodice. For those who dared, it was wearable every day.

Leaving Las Vegas (1995) is known for having Westwood's name attached, even though there is little of her work in the finished picture. Kudos has to be given to costumier Laura Goldsmith for the film's look; Westwood was only specifically responsible for the short skirts and corset tops worn by Elisabeth Shue as prostitute Sera. Her skirts are nappa leather, restrictively tight so explicitly sexy, and sitting on the natural waistline. The so-called corset tops are actually bustiers, and relatively simple ones at that. In a nutshell, a corset is long enough to cinch in the waist and hips; they are generally metal- or whale-boned and laced up from the rear. Bustiers are far more common garments; they are cheaper to produce and easier to wear because the structure consists of a flexible stretchy fabric. Corsets can either include a bra or fit directly under the bust. A bustier will always include a bra.

Elisabeth Shue wears V-shaped bustiers in Leaving Las Vegas that are designed to be outerwear. The inference is obviously sexual, with the direction of the V pointing directly towards Sera's crotch. A corset functions as an undergarment – it is designed to train and hold the form in an impossible silhouette – but the bustier is almost entirely fashion. Sera's black bustier top with shock red leather skirt glimpsed as she visits her pimp is most indicative of Westwood's input. The V is so pronounced it almost gives the impression of an unfastened all-in-one body with the snaps removed. Westwood only agreed to become involved in Leaving Las Vegas because the director, Mike Figgis, once went to school with her son. By and large, movies have done nothing but disappoint the designer. She was so incensed with how director Derek Jarman misrepresented punk in Jubilee (1978) that she made a T-shirt expressing the fact.

Although it is said that Westwood is a fan of Leaving Las Vegas, she certainly did not think much of the first Sex and the City movie (2008). Her custom-designed wedding gown, made of ivory silk satin with built-in corset, becomes intrinsic to the plot when bride-to-be Carrie (Sarah Jessica Parker) is delivered the dress by hand, supposedly donated by Westwood because she is the only one who should wear it. Ultimately Carrie rejects the garment to get married in a plain vintage suit. This is probably the first time Sex and the City has denounced high fashion for the empty spectacle it often is. The audience did not approve, and neither did Vivienne Westwood, who left the premiere early with nothing complimentary to say about the

film's costume designer, Patricia Field. Incidentally,
due to the popularity of Westwood's dress, her London
boutique offered the gown on special order for a limited
time, and online retailer Net-a-Porter released a similar
version the following year.

Proving she has a sense of humour, Westwood
agreed to provide four ensembles, including a Harris
Tweed suit and wedding dress, for Miss Piggy in trave-
logue caper Muppets Most Wanted (2014). Westwood
insisted on designing all of the ensembles Miss Piggy
wears while in London. Costumier Rahel Afiley had
wanted Stella McCartney to create Miss Piggy's outfits,
but from a marketing perspective Westwood was still
the bigger name. Very little was altered by Afiley, except
for the wedding gown, which arrived from Westwood's
team shaped more for a human body than for Miss
Piggy's specific proportions. Afiley also requested that
the fabric be re-dyed cream instead of white – far more
suitable for Miss Piggy's character. As all costume
designers know, movie clothes are not fashion, they are
costume. Even when the benefits of involving a fashion
designer are sought, everything they contribute must
ultimately fit the context of the story.

YVES SAINT LAURENT

THE PINK PANTHER (1963)
BELLE DE JOUR (1968)
MISSISSIPPI MERMAID (1969)

Yves Saint Laurent sketching designs in 1960. Saint Laurent's constant innovation and blurring of gender boundaries make him one of the greatest designers of all time
—
p216 Catherine Deneuve wearing an ostrich-feather-trimmed coat in *Mississippi Mermaid*, exemplifying her character's disregard of the need to 'lay low'

At his height during the sixties and seventies, Yves Saint Laurent was just as likely to be seen in gossip magazines as near a catwalk. His relationship with cinema consisted mainly of creating costumes for muse Catherine Deneuve, whom he met in 1965. Hailed a 'genius' by tastemaker Diana Vreeland, Saint Laurent presented collections that toyed with stereotype convention, especially with regards to androgyny. His 'Le Smoking', essentially a feminine tuxedo, launched an era of contoured trouser suits for women that continues today, and is now seen as the pinnacle of a fascinating, always experimental career.

The Pink Panther (1963) was Saint Laurent's first film credit. Officially he designed costumes for Capucine and Claudia Cardinale, although Russian designer Princess Irene Galitzine provided Cardinale's white tunic and pants ensemble. Cardinale plays a princess in the movie, ethnically styled for the fictitious Middle Eastern country Lugash. Capucine is most obviously styled by Saint Laurent, in sleek coats and softly draped dresses that swathe her body rather than contort it. Capucine's reversible wool coat with detachable puritan collar is probably more a contribution of costumier Annalisa Nasalli-Rocca than Saint Laurent, but the amount of Saint Laurent's work featured in *The Pink Panther* is hardly relevant: the film brought him international attention just three years after resigning as chief designer at Christian Dior. Smaller-scale productions followed, including dressing Jean Seberg for *Moment to Moment* (1965). However, it was *Belle de Jour* (1968) that established Saint Laurent – already popular as a fashion designer – in the movie world.

Catherine Deneuve plays outwardly conservative housewife Séverine in *Belle de Jour*. Characterized by her clinically neat attire, Séverine begins exploring her latent sexual desires by selling her body at a brothel. Her appearance gradually comes undone the more fervently she welcomes these desires. Saint Laurent dressed Deneuve in variations of the garment that established his career – a reworking of the sailor's pea coat. Séverine is fastened into a red-breasted skirt suit (signifying the 'scarlet woman'), a brown leather princess-line coat, a grey mid-length double-breasted woollen coat, and a black PVC tunic – all sporting rows of decorative buttons and symbolic of Séverine's military-like repression. The unstructured flared shift she wears on her first visit to the brothel appears to suggest freedom but in fact denotes just how vulnerable and unprotected she is. Her Saint Laurent clothes are not armour, they are uniform. Without them, she is finally free to embrace her true self.

Mississippi Mermaid (*La sirène du Mississipi*, 1969), Yves Saint Laurent's third on-screen collaboration with Catherine Deneuve, explores similar themes to *Belle de Jour*. Deneuve plays Julie, an apparently homely girl who dupes millionaire Louis Mahé (Jean-Paul Belmondo) into thinking she is his 'correspondence bride', then steals all his money. Louis pursues Julie, confronts her, but realizes he is enraptured. A hopeless love affair plays out, with Julie's metamorphosis into femme fatale charted by her wardrobe. Julie constructs her persona as a phoney wife with modish Saint Laurent ensembles: a safari skirt suit (echoing the shirt in which Saint Laurent dressed model Veruschka for a 1968 *Vogue* shoot), an asymmetric A-line skirt with thick leather belt, silk shirts and a plain blue sweater. Reflecting Deneuve's simple chic of the sixties, and Saint Laurent's best-remembered look, Julie's outfits show no flash, played down as if to imply her suppressed guilt. She fights the allure of couture, but only when she has money. When she and Louis run short, Julie yearns for a spectacular coat trimmed in ostrich feathers. Here Saint Laurent turns the idea of cool couture on its head. Julie hides in sedate taupe shifts and roll-necks, only to come alive in an exhibitionist coat that figuratively exposes her deceit.

Yves Saint Laurent's connection with Catherine Deneuve continued in cinema, with the likes of camp horror *The Hunger* (1983), swapping taupe linen A-lines for black leather pencil skirts. *Belle de Jour*, however, remains one of the greatest fashion films ever made, and Saint Laurent's best work is remembered on screen.

p218 Capucine (left) and Claudia Cardinale (right) on the set of *The Pink Panther*. Both were 'principally dressed' by Saint Laurent

—

p219 top left Sketch of Catherine Deneuve's grey wool double-breasted coat in *Belle du Jour*

—

p219 top right Deneuve as Séverine, the 'scarlet woman', in red Saint Laurent coat and matching princess-cut dress in *Belle du Jour*

—

p219 bottom left Catherine Deneuve in a wrapover A-line skirt for *Mississippi Mermaid*, an immensely flattering Saint Laurent staple still produced by the brand today

—

p219 bottom right The A-line skirt is still a feature of Yves Saint Laurent's contemporary collections, seen here in the Autumn/Winter 2015. The platform shoes and floral-print shirt are another obvious reference to the late 1960s

INDEX

Figures in **bold** refer to main entries;
figures in *italics* refer to illustrations;
(c) refers to captions

PICTURE CREDITS

Laurence King Publishing, the author, and the picture researchers wish to thank the institutions and individuals who have kindly provided photographic material for use in this book. While every effort has been made to trace the present copyright holders we apologize in advance for any unintentional omission or error and will be pleased to insert the appropriate acknowledgements in any subsequent edition.

Front cover
Moviestore Collection/REX/Shutterstock

Back cover
Left: MGM/Columbia/EON/The Kobal Collection; top right: The Kobal Collection; bottom right: Paramount/The Kobal Collection.

Page 7 © Kurt and Bart; 8 Live Entertainment/The Kobal Collection; 9 Courtesy of Agnes B, photographer: Patrick Swirc; 10t Delpire Prods/The Kobal Collection; 10b Courtesy of Agnes B; 11l © William Klein; 11r Victor VIRGILE/Gamma-Rapho via Getty Images; 12l Miramax/Buena Vista/The Kobal Collection; 12r Miramax/Buena Vista; 13 Courtesy Everett Collection/REX Shutterstock; 14 Victor VIRGILE/Gamma-Rapho via Getty Images; 15 © Jacques Pavlovsky/Sygma/Corbis; 16l, 16r Sharok Hatami/REX Shutterstock; 17 20th Century Fox/The Kobal Collection; 18 Photo @ AGIP/Bridgeman Images; 18 S.N.C./Tritone/The Kobal Collection; 19 Paramount Pictures/The Kobal Collection; 20 Danjaq/EON/UA/The Kobal Collection; 21 SIPA PRESS/REX Shutterstock; 22l, 22r Danjaq/EON/UA/The Kobal Collection; 23l © AF archive/Alamy Stock Photo; 23r Paisley Park Films/Warner Bros/The Kobal Collection; 24 RKO/The Kobal Collection/John Miehle; 25 Bettmann/Getty Images; 26t RKO/The Kobal Collection; 26b © Moviestore collection Ltd/Alamy Stock Photo; 27 Columbia/The Kobal Collection; 28 20th Century Fox/The Kobal Collection/Barry Wetcher; 29 Shelly Katz/The LIFE Images Collection/Getty Images; 30 © United Archives GmbH/Alamy Stock Photo; 30r Indianapolis Museum of Art, USA/Gift of Mr. Bill Blass/Bridgeman Images. © estate of Bill Blass; 31 Follow Through Productions/Salamander Pictures/Laura Ziskin Productions/The Kobal Collection; 32 Bazmark Films/The Kobal Collection; 33 Al Seib/Los Angeles Times via Getty Images; 34 Universal Pictures/The Kobal Collection; 35 Warner Bros. Pictures/The Kobal Collection; 36 Paramount/The Kobal Collection; 37 Waring Abbott/Getty Images; 38t, 38b Paramount/The Kobal Collection; 39 20th Century Fox/The Kobal Collection/Barry Wetcher; 40 Paramount/The Kobal Collection; 41 Tunbridge-Sedgwick Pictorial Press/Getty Images; 42t Associated Newspapers/REX Shutterstock; 42b Warner Bros. Pictures/The Kobal Collection; 43 © Christie's Images/Corbis. © National Portrait Gallery, London; 44 Courtesy Everett Collection/REX Shutterstock/TopFoto; 45 The Granger Collection/TopFoto; 46l Dress by Christian Dior, 1948 (New Look style)/Bridgeman Images; 46r Ken Ishii/Getty Images for Dior; 47 Universal/The Kobal Collection; 48 Courtesy Everett Collection/REX Shutterstock; 49 © Everett Collection Historical/Alamy Stock Photo; 50l Courtesy Everett Collection/REX Shutterstock; 50r © Rue des Archives/Tallandier/Lebrecht Collection; 51 Goldwyn/United Artists/The Kobal Collection; 52 Columbia/The Kobal Collection; 53 Susan Wood/Getty Images; 54 Victor VIRGILE/Gamma-Rapho via Getty Images; 55t Columbia/The Kobal Collection; 55b Atlas Entertainment/The Kobal Collection; 56 © AF archive/Alamy Stock Photo; 57 Victor Boyko/DolceGabbana/Getty Images for Dolce&Gabbana and Moda; 58 20th Century Fox/The Kobal Collection/Merrick Morton;

59t 20th Century Fox/The Kobal Collection/K C Bailey; 59b El Deseo S.A./The Kobal Collection; 60 ©20th Century Fox/Everett/REX Shutterstock; 61 Rose Hartman/Getty Images; 62 Courtesy of Donna Karan; 63l Victor VIRGILE/Gamma-Rapho via Getty Images; 63r 20th Century Fox/The Kobal Collection/Barry Wetcher; 64 © AF archive/Alamy Stock Photo; 65 Nina Leen/The LIFE Picture Collection/Getty Images; 66l Courtesy of Elsa Schiaparelli; 66r © Mary Evans Picture Library/Alamy Stock Photo; 67l, 67r Paramount/The Kobal Collection; 68t United Artists/Getty Images; 68b The Margaret Herrick Collection; 69 United Artists/Getty Images; 70 Columbia/The Kobal Collection; 71 ©ullsteinbild/TopFoto; 72l Rusconi/Gaumont/The Kobal Collection; 72r Touchstone Pictures/The Kobal Collection/James Hamilton; 73l © AF archive/Alamy Stock Photo; 73r © Fairchild Photo Service/Condé Nast/Corbis; 74, 75 MGM/The Kobal Collection; 76l MGM/The Kobal Collection/George Hurrell; 76r MGM/The Kobal Collection/Laszlo Willinger; 77 MGM/The Kobal Collection/George Hurrell; 78 © Pictorial Press Ltd/Alamy Stock Photo; 79 MGM/The Kobal Collection; 80 © CinemaPhoto/Corbis; 81 © David Lees/Corbis; 82l Ardustry Entertainment/The Kobal Collection; 82r Appian Way/Paramount/The Kobal Collection; 83 Before The Door/Washington Square Films/A24/Old Bull Pictures/The Kobal Collection/Atsushi Nishijima; 84 Imagine Entertainment/The Kobal Collection; 85 John Minihan/Evening Standard/Getty Images; 86 Imagine Entertainment/The Kobal Collection; 87, 88 Atlas Entertainment/The Kobal Collection; 89 Michael Evans/Getty Images; 90 Moviestore/REX Shutterstock; 91 Agoes Rudianto/Anadolu Agency/Getty Images; 91 Atlas Entertainment/The Kobal Collection; 92 © Glasshouse Images/Alamy Stock Photo; 93 Popperfoto/Getty Images; 94t 20th Century Fox/The Kobal Collection; 94b Kirstin Sinclair/Getty Images; 95 MGM/Stanley Kubrick Productions/The Kobal Collection; 96 MGM/The Kobal Collection; 97 Courtesy of Christian Esquevin; 98t, 98c, 99 MGM/The Kobal Collection; 100 Gravier Prods/Perdido Productions/The Kobal Collection; 101 Photo © Tallandier/Bridgeman Images; 102t Edward R. Pressman Film/The Kobal Collection; 102b Startraks Photo/REX Shutterstock; 103t © AF archive/Alamy Stock Photo; 103b Touchstone Pictures/The Kobal Collection; 104 RKO/The Kobal Collection; 105 Courtesy Christian Esquevin; 106 Paramount/The Kobal Collection; 107t RKO/The Kobal Collection; 107b Pascal Le Segretain/Getty Images; 108 Paramount/The Kobal Collection/Bud Fraker; 109 © Eric Robert/Sygma/Corbis; 110t Paramount/The Kobal Collection; 110bl Pascal Le Segretain/Getty Images; 110br Edith Head/Private Collection/Photo © Christie's Images/Bridgeman Images. © Motion Picture and Television Fund; 111l, 111r Universal/The Kobal Collection; 112 20th Century Fox/The Kobal Collection; 113l Courtesy Everett Collection/REX Shutterstock; 113r © United Archives GmbH/Alamy Stock Photo; 114 United Artists/The Kobal Collection/Bob Coburn; 115 Alfred Eisenstaedt/Pix Inc./The LIFE Picture Collection/Getty Images; 116 Courtesy Everett Collection/REX Shutterstock; 117 Studio Canal/The Kobal Collection; 118 Columbia/The Kobal Collection/Frank Cronenweth; 119 John Kobal Foundation/Getty Images; 120l, 120r Universal/The Kobal Collection; 121 © AF archive/Alamy Stock Photo; 122 El Deseo/Ciby 2000/The Kobal Collection; 123 © Trinity Mirror/Mirrorpix/Alamy Stock Photo; 124l Alain BENAINOUS/Gamma-Rapho via Getty Images; 124r Jeff Kravitz/AMA2009/FilmMagic/Getty Images; 125 Columbia/Tri-Star/The Kobal Collection; 126t Columbia/Tri-Star/The Kobal Collection/Jack English; 126b Jun Sato/WireImage/Getty Images; 127 El Deseo S.A./The Kobal Collection; 128 UPI/Canal+ Espana/El Deseo/The Kobal Collection; 129 Keystone-France/Gamma-Keystone via Getty Images; 131tl © Moviestore collection Ltd/Alamy Stock Photo; 131tr © epa european presssphoto agency b.v./Alamy Stock Photo; 131br Betzer-Panorama Film/Danish Film Inst/The Kobal Collection; 132 Morgan Creek/The Kobal Collection; 133 REX Shutterstock; 134l Warner Bros./The Kobal Collection; 134r © Kurt and Bart; 135 Fox Searchlight Pictures/The Kobal Collection; 136 Columbia/American Zoetrope/Sony/The Kobal Collection; 137 Ian Cook/The LIFE Images Collection/Getty Images; 138l, 138r Courtesy of Manolo Blahnik; 139t Columbia/American Zoetrope/Sony/The Kobal Collection; 139b Courtesy of Manolo Blahnik;

140 Fox Searchlight/The Kobal Collection; 141 Victor VIRGILE/Gamma-Rapho via Getty Images; 142 Fox Searchlight/The Kobal Collection; 143l LD Entertainment/The Kobal Collection/Phil Bray; 143r Peter Michael Dills/Getty Images; 144 © William Klein; 145 © Everett Collection Historical/Alamy Stock Photo; 146tl Courtesy Everett Collection/REX Shutterstock; 146tr Bryanston/The Kobal Collection; 146br © Museum of London. Courtesy of Dame Mary Quant; 147l, 147r Columbia Pictures/Getty Images; 148 Paramount/The Kobal Collection; 149 Courtesy of Nino Cerruti; 150 Touchstone Pictures/The Kobal Collection; 151l © AF archive/Alamy Stock Photo; 151r Columbia/Tri-Star/The Kobal Collection; 152 © AF archive/Alamy Stock Photo; 153 Photo © Gerald Bloncourt/Bridgeman Images; 154l THOMAS COEX/AFP/Getty Images; 154r Charley Hel/Prestige/Getty Images; 155l © AF archive/Alamy Stock Photo; 155r Paramount/The Kobal Collection; 156 20th Century Fox/The Kobal Collection; 157 Popperfoto/Getty Images; 158l © Pictorial Press Ltd/Alamy Stock Photo; 158r Courtesy Cocinor/Ronald Grant Archive; 159 © AF archive/Alamy Stock Photo; 160t MGM/Photofest; 160b © Illustrated London News/Mary Evans; 161l, 161r © AF archive/Alamy Stock Photo; 162 Courtesy Everett Collection/REX Shutterstock; 163 © Manuel Litran/Corbis; 164 Courtesy DisCina/Ronald Grant Archive; 165l Bill Eppridge/The LIFE Picture Collection/Getty Images; 165r Kristy Sparow/Getty Images; 166 Bazmark Films/The Kobal Collection; 167 Courtesy of Prada; 168l MGM/Columbia/EON/The Kobal Collection; 168r © Heineken; 169 20th Century Fox/The Kobal Collection; 170 First Sun/Mikado Film/The Kobal Collection; 171 Billy Farrell/BFAnyc.com/REX Shutterstock; 172 First Sun/Mikado Film/The Kobal Collection; 173 © Photos 12/Alamy Stock Photo; 174 Paramount/Photofest; 175 Susan Wood/Getty Images; 176 Moviestore/REX/Shutterstock; 177 United Artists/Rollins-Joffe/The Kobal Collection/Brian Hamill; 178 Fox Searchlight/The Kobal Collection; 179 Courtesy of Amy Westcott; 180l Rob Loud/Getty Images; 180r Courtesy of Amy Westcott; 181 Fox Searchlight/The Kobal Collection; 182 20th Century Fox/Bazmark Films/The Kobal Collection; 183 Mondadori Portfolio via Getty Images; 184 © Granamour Weems Collection/Alamy Stock Photo; 185t Imagine Entertainment/The Kobal Collection; 185b Courtesy of Salvatore Ferragamo; 186 Paramount/The Kobal Collection; 187, 188 Courtesy of Kevin Conran; 189t, 189b Paramount/The Kobal Collection; 190 Universal/The Kobal Collection/Bob Penn; 191 ©TopFoto.co.uk; 192 MGM/The Kobal Collection; 193l Henry Clarke/Condé Nast via Getty Images; 193r © Fred Prouser/Reuters; 194 MGM/Columbia/EON/The Kobal Collection; 195 Courtesy Fade to Black/Ronald Grant Archive; 196 MGM/Columbia/EON/The Kobal Collection; 197t Danjaq/EON Productions/The Kobal Collection; 197b Columbia/EON/Danjaq/MGM/The Kobal Collection/Stephen Vaughan; 198 Paramount/The Kobal Collection/E.R. Richee; 199 Courtesy Everett Collection/REX Shutterstock; 200 Courtesy Paramount/Ronald Grant Archive; 201 Paramount/The Kobal Collection/E.R. Richee; 202l, 202r, 203 Courtesy Everett Collection/REX Shutterstock; 204 New Regency Pictures/The Kobal Collection; 205 Andrew Toth/Getty Images; 206t Regency Entertainment/The Kobal Collection; 206b, 207 New Regency Pictures/The Kobal Collection; 208 Eon/Danjaq/Sony/The Kobal Collection; 209 Angelo Deligio/Mondadori Portfolio via Getty Images; 210t El Deseo/CIBY 2000/The Kobal Collection; 210b MGM/EON/The Kobal Collection/Keith Hamshere; 211l Chockstone Pictures/The Kobal Collection; 211r Appian Way/Paramount/The Kobal Collection; 212 United Artists/Courtesy Eve/REX/Shutterstock; 213 Mike Marsland/WireImage; 214l Anglo International/The Kobal Collection; 214r New Line Cinema/The Kobal Collection; 215 Walt Disney Pictures/Mandeville Films/Babieka/Cinema Vehicle Services/The Kobal Collection; 216 The Kobal Collection; 217 © Photos 12/Alamy Stock Photo; 218 United Artists/The Kobal Collection; 219tl © Fondation Pierre Bergé – Yves Saint Laurent, Paris; 219tr Paris Film/Five Film/The Kobal Collection; 219bl © ScreenProd/Photononstop/Alamy Stock Photo; 219br Antonio de Moraes Barros Filho/WireImage/Getty Images.